LINCOLN CHRISTIAN COLLEGE

Business Thinking

in Not-for-Profit Organizations

Gail Walraven

Chief Operating Officer
The Whittier Institute
Scripps Institutions of Medicine and Science
La Jolla, California

 AN ASPEN PUBLICATION®
Aspen Publishers, Inc.
Gaithersburg, Maryland
1995

This publication is designed to provide accurate and authoritative information in regard to the Subject Matter covered. It is sold with the understanding that the publisher is not engaged in rendering legal, accounting, or other professional service. If legal advice or other expert assistance is required, the service of a competent professional person should be sought. (From a Declaration of Principles jointly adopted by a Committee of the American Bar Association and a Committee of Publishers and Associations.)

Library of Congress Cataloging-in-Publication Data

Walraven, Gail, 1949–
Business thinking in not-for-profit organizations/Gail Walraven
p.   cm.
Includes bibliographical references and index.
ISBN: 0-8342-0424-X
1. Nonprofit organizations—Management. I. Title.
HD62.6.W35 1995
658'.82'048—dc20
94-20974
CIP

Copyright © 1995 by Aspen Publishers, Inc.
All rights reserved.

Names of products, providers, organizations, and businesses, as well as case studies, examples, data charts, and other quantitative material used in this book to illustrate content, have been altered to the extent necessary to protect confidentiality of the sources.

None of the financial indicators is in any way a reflection of the financial performance of any individual institution.

Aspen Publishers, Inc., grants permission for photocopying for limited personal or internal use. This consent does not extend to other kinds of copying, such as copying for general distribution, for advertising or promotional purposes, for creating new collective works, or for resale. For information, address Aspen Publishers, Inc., Permissions Department, 200 Orchard Ridge Drive, Gaithersburg, Maryland 20878.

Editorial Resources: Ruth Bloom

Library of Congress Catalog Card Number: 94-20974
ISBN: 0-8342-0424-X

Printed in the United States of America

1   2   3   4   5

Table of Contents

Introduction vii
    End of an Era viii
    The Profit Mandate viii
    The "P Word" ix
    How to Use This Book x
    Questions on the Introduction xi

1—Business Definition 1
    Mission Statement 3
    Business Clarity 5
    Vision 6
    Corporate Identity 7
    Profit Obligation 8
    Questions on Chapter 1: Business Definition 11

2—Products and Product Lines 13
    Product Line Profitability 13
    Determining Your Products 14
    Analyzing Product Profitability 15
    Acting on Product Profitability 16
    Questions on Chapter 2: Products and Product Lines 17

3—Profit Formula 19
    Profit Accountability 19
    What Is the Profit Formula? 20
    How the Profit Formula Works 20
    Applying the Profit Formula 24
    Reporting Profit Variables 27

96832

Just a Note on Data 28
Analyzing Product Profit 28
Questions on Chapter 3: Profit Formula 35

4—Minizing Costs 37
Figuring Out Costs 37
Cost Vocabulary 38
Cost Detail 44
Cost Measures 45
Calculating Cost 46
Influencing Cost 48
Conclusion 49
Questions on Chapter 4: Minimizing Costs 50

5—Maximizing Revenues 53
Terminology 53
Revenue in a Not-for-Profit World 54
Measures of Reimbursement 54
Payer Categories 55
Revenue Types 55
Influencing Revenue 56
Unit Profitability 63
Questions on Chapter 5: Maximizing Revenue 64

6—Increasing Sales Volume 67
Principles of Profitability 67
Not-for-Profit Sales Functions 67
Ways To Increase Sales Volume 68
Marketing and the Marketplace 70
Market Research 74
Who Are Your Customers 74
Who Is the Competition? 77
Product Portfolio 80
Strategic Marketing Plan 83
The Marketing Plan 86
Sales Plan 89
Conclusion 90
Questions on Chapter 6: Increasing Sales Volume 91

7—Monitoring Performance **97**
 Goals of Financial Reporting 97
 Accompanying Notes 108
 Trend Reporting 109
 Trend Variables 110
 Questions on Chapter 7: Monitoring Performance 113

8—Return on Investment **117**
 Concept of ROI 117
 Calculating ROI 118
 Profitability 122
 Questions on Chapter 8: Return on Investment 123

Index **125**

—— ❧ ——

Introduction

Generally speaking, organizations are divided into two types: "for-profit" and "not-for-profit." The for-profit companies are readily recognized: they are the IBMs®, McDonald's®, and Wal-Marts® of the world. For-profit businesses are created with the expectation of making money; they are in business with the obligation of making more money than they spend. They expect to cover their costs and have some money left over, which they call profit.

In the not-for-profit (NFP) arena are all of the governmental agencies, such as the post office and the school system, and the private not-for-profits, such as charitable organizations, hospitals, and civic groups. But what makes an organization not-for-profit? What does that term mean? Does it mean that the organization didn't make any money last year? Or that it made money but wasn't supposed to? Or that it made money but didn't tell the Internal Revenue Service (IRS)? Or what?

Not-for-profit companies aren't expected to make a profit; in fact, they are sometimes called nonprofits. Most people are happy if not-for-profit companies just break even (this being a lofty goal for many of them). They want to make enough money to cover expenses, but they don't want a lot of profit to call attention to their tax-exempt status. When an NFP happens to make a profit, it's not called profit. It's called a "surplus," "excess reserves," or an "operating gain."

For-profit companies take their profit and distribute it to key people: the shareholders, investors, etc. If a not-for-profit company makes money, it is expected (at least by the IRS) to reinvest its profit back into the company, rather than paying it out to others.

END OF AN ERA

In the past, there was another very big difference between for-profit and not-for-profit companies. The for-profit companies lived or died according to how well they managed their businesses. There was a certain justice to watching the corner convenience store fail because its prices were too high. But the not-for-profit organizations always seemed to survive, no matter how inefficient or disorganized they were. If the post office needed more money, it just raised the price of stamps. The schools or health care system just took a bigger bite of taxes. Mental health centers wrote for more grants, charged more fees, or held more fund-raisers. The world went on, and the not-for-profit organizations continued to function inefficiently because they were subsidized, often by the public at large in the form of taxes.

Then something dramatic happened. The taxpayers revolted and began refusing to give blank-check subsidies. They set limits on the amount of money they would pay, and the not-for-profits began to notice a change in their world. They no longer had unlimited funds, they no longer were able to go about "business as usual," and many lifelong institutions were actually at risk of failing because of their inability to reduce their costs to stay within the new revenue limits. We've seen public schools declaring bankruptcy, museums selling off collections or staying open fewer hours, public mail services losing market share, and health care providers closing their doors—all because their operations had never been set up to keep their costs in line with their revenues.

THE PROFIT MANDATE

In today's environment, every business must make a profit. This is particularly difficult for the not-for-profits, who have always been told not even to say the word *profit* for fear of evoking IRS ire. Now, without the guarantee of unlimited subsidies, they must learn the "*P* word," even if they call it an operating gain, and they must produce a surplus to survive.

There is a new imperative in the world of not-for-profit companies to restructure their businesses with this profit mandate. Within each business, management must embrace the "*P* word," understand how it works, and set up their business units to ensure profitability.

THE "*P* WORD"

In any business, the profitability margin resides at the lower levels of the organizational structure. Both costs and revenues are affected most directly at the points where the product is produced and where it meets the customer. The employees at these levels must have such comfort with the "*P* word" that they can intuitively manipulate operations to enhance profit.

For example, in public parks and recreation departments, the front-line employees often influence the initial purchase choice with their technical opinions—that initial purchase decision greatly affects both initial and ongoing costs. Then they have tremendous impact on equipment costs in the way they treat and maintain the equipment. Front-line workers are often in the best position to recommend ideas for collecting revenues to cover expenses, and possible new service ideas or new revenue sources, such as park day use fees, to provide excess revenue (profit) to expand their future service. The principle is the same regardless of the type of organization. It applies to staffers who maintain summer programs for the YMCA/YWCA . . . or day-care, latchkey, or adult education in public schools . . . or an employee assistance program marketed by a mental health agency. If employees at all levels of the business are made aware of profit and recognize how they influence it, they can change the entire financial picture of the organization as a whole.

One very effective way to ensure this mind-set is to set up each department of the NFP as if it were a free-standing for-profit business. Under the direction of the middle manager, that business unit should formulate its mission statement; define its products and product lines; calculate costs, reimbursement, and margins for its products; profile its markets and customers; position it to compete; strategize its expansion; monitor and report on margins and trends; and demonstrate its overall return on investment.

The purpose of this book is to provide a methodical process for building departments into businesses. It will give managers the infrastructure needed for step-by-step business planning. But more than that, it offers for-profit business strategies for thinking and acting in a not-for-profit world.

HOW TO USE THIS BOOK

To use this book, each department manager should begin by defining the exact nature of the business of that department. As you read through Chapter 1, consider your business to be the activities and mandates of the department you represent within your organization. The issues raised and questions presented should refer to your department within your not-for-profit organization. Your challenge is to see your department in an entirely new light—as a for-profit company that is responsible for its own revenues and in charge of its own future. Be creative and entrepreneurial! You are defining a new business structure and building a new workplace for yourself and your employees. Your efforts will determine in large part the success of your entire organization in tomorrow's world.

———

Note: The terms *product* and *service* are used interchangeably throughout this text, as are the terms *business, company, organization,* and *institution*. Although there are distinct differences in these terms, they are alike for the purposes of this subject.

QUESTIONS ON THE INTRODUCTION

1. Write down the name of your not-for-profit organization.

2. Decide whether you will be managing the profitability of the entire organization, or just a piece of it, such as one or more departments. For example, if you are the executive director of the AIDS Awareness Foundation, you will be responsible for the profitability of the entire foundation. If you are the financial manager of a cancer research institute, you might focus only on the accounting department, or you might decide that, for purposes of this book, you want to examine the profitability of the entire institute. Think about this for a minute. Then write down exactly what you will be focusing on in this book, and what you won't.

*   *   *

Now you're ready to go on to Chapter 1.

1

Business Definition

Imagine that you have just gone into business for yourself. You've rented a small storefront down on Main Street, and the painters are coming tomorrow to paint the signs on your front windows.

What would you have them paint? What does your company do or sell or provide or produce? Is your product attractive enough to entice anyone to enter your store? Would they pay for the product you are selling? Will enough people come in and pay to make it worth your time and expenses to keep the doors open?

These are not easy questions to answer for a not-for-profit organization. It's often hard to visualize your services all lined up on a shelf. For instance, what does a hospital sell? Or an elementary school? Or a fire department? Or the public library? How about the YMCA, or the department of motor vehicles, or the Cancer Society? What business are these operations in? What do they sell? Who buys what they sell?

These are the basic questions of business. Before you can begin counting your profits, you must be very clear about what business you're in and what it is that you provide to the customer. You should begin to define these things for the not-for-profit business you represent. Once you can answer these key questions, you can begin to control your profitability.

For the NFP to become profitable, the NFP manager must also be a business manager. This means that the existing manager (museum's department head, day-care program director, school

1

Storefront on Main Street

department chair, local government agency supervisor, etc.) must take a growing interest in the business aspects of his or her area of responsibility. The NFP could have a number of business managers, each of whom is responsible for the profitability of a separate department. It's up to each NFP manager to become a business manager with the knowledge and skills needed to improve profitability.

MISSION STATEMENT

Start with the mission statement. What is the purpose of your business (your department)? Let's say you run the finance department of the school district. Is it your business to construct the budget, or to meet the financial needs of your customers (the individual schools)? If you run the art museum, is your business to house the city's art resources, or to display art, or to preserve art, or to teach

Mission Statement

- ## Clarifies
- ## Focuses
- ## Commits
- ## Communicates
- ## Markets

art, or all of these? Or is it something bigger, such as fostering an appreciation of art?

You should give serious and ample thought to your mission. You must be clear on the purpose of your business before you can run it successfully. The purpose you settle on will ultimately guide all of your future business decisions.

Mission
Vision
Values

- Should answer the question, "Why do we exist?"

- Should be written from the customer's perspective

- Should be simple, yet elegant

- Should inspire to greatness!

When your purpose is clear in your own mind, you're ready to write your mission statement. This should be a brief, succinct synopsis of why you're in business. It should answer the question, "Why do we exist?" The mission statement clarifies and focuses your thinking about your business purpose. Beyond that, it commits you to your purpose and communicates that purpose to your employees, your customers, and the world at large. Effectively constructed, a good mission statement can be a very powerful marketing tool.

Write your mission statement from the customer's perspective. It should be simple, but elegant, and should inspire your staff to greatness. Exhibit 1–1 shows a number of sample mission statements. Some are great and some aren't as good, but each has elements that communicate the feeling of the business.

Don't confuse your mission with your capabilities. A gas station might be in business to sell gas, but it can also change tires. The spectrum of capability extends infinitely from the core of the business (its mission) to the distant horizon of marginal ability. For example, the mission of a school might be to educate children, but the school might also be capable of providing day care or adult education. A mental health agency might have a mission of providing acute care and also be capable of training the community in prevention of mental health problems.

It's the job of the business manager to clarify the mission and determine the capabilities. A good business manager knows where to draw the line in order to retain effective business focus. If the parks and recreation department takes up mowing neighborhood lawns just because it is capable of doing so, it could seriously jeopardize its ability to focus on its real mission. The boundaries you draw around your business could be the difference between doing things well and doing all things. The most effective businesses are those that know how to stick to their knitting.

BUSINESS CLARITY

As a business manager you must have crystal clarity around what you sell, what you advertise, and what you make money on. They're not always the same thing. The cafeteria sells sandwiches,

Exhibit 1–1 Sample Mission Statements

San Diego Zoo Dedicated to Increasing Understanding and Appreciation of the Inherent Worth of All Life Forms by Exhibiting Animals and Plants in Natural Settings and Applying Its Efforts and Influences to the Conservation of the Earth's Wildlife	SAFETY • RESPONSIBILITY • SECURITY SRS Savannah River Site The Mission of the Savannah River Site is to serve the national security interest of the United States by safely producing nuclear materials while protecting the employee and public health and the environment
Mercy HEART INSTITUTE The mission of the Mercy Heart Institute is to provide the most comprehensive, state-of-the-art cardiovascular health care services available today, thereby promoting total cardiovascular health, both for individuals and for the community at large.	The Starship ENTERPRISE ...to explore new worlds, discover new civilizations, seek out new life forms, and to boldly go where no one has gone before.

but it advertises clean, fast service, and makes its money on the soft drinks.

It's okay that your customers don't make this distinction, but it's unforgivable for your managers to confuse these key elements.

VISION

The business manager must have a clear mental picture of the organization's goals and objectives, and vivid visual images of suc-

Mission Capabilities Zone

cess. This vision should be larger than life, and should fill the workers with enthusiasm and energy. A vivid vision, effectively communicated with analogies and illustrations, engages the work force and fills it with the same motivation that drives the leader to build the company.

CORPORATE IDENTITY

Once you're clear on your business purpose, mission, and vision, only then can you begin to construct your corporate identity. You want to create an external image that communicates your vision and purpose to the outside world. Your choice of name, slogan, logo, letterhead, business cards, and the like, together make up your corporate identity package.

Take a look at Exhibit 1–2, which shows a page from the local phone directory. Here we have identical services that differentiate

Exhibit 1–2 Escort Service Image Ads

themselves with very simple ads reflecting what they perceive to be their corporate identity. You must admit that the ads immediately give a clear visual picture of what you could expect from each of these businesses.

PROFIT OBLIGATION

By now you're probably asking yourself why you should care about profit. Many NFPs believe that profit is irrelevant to them and is something they probably shouldn't even want. But think of profit as excess revenue. This is the money you will use next year. It's the money you have left after you pay your expenses. If you look at it that way, it has clear value, and the more you have of it, the more you are able to invest in your programs and grow.

If you still can't see the value of profit, consider this: All NFPs know how hard it is to raise money. Fund development is one of the greatest challenges NFPs face. Think of profit as a head start on fund-raising. The more profit you have for next year, the less philanthropic support you'll need.

Profit...

...is the seed corn of business. If you eat all you grow, you'll be out of business next year.

Profit is an obligation of doing business. All businesses have an obligation to make a profit. If an organization consistently spends in excess of its revenues, it cannot remain open for long. Not only is it okay for NFPs to make a profit, it's smart business for them to be profitable so that they can reinvest in their future programs.

In every business, every worker has a role in profit management. In NFP businesses, it is especially difficult for those on the line to appreciate the importance of and the formula for making a profit. But the organization as a whole cannot expect to be profitable unless its entire work force operates in profit-making ways.

QUESTIONS ON CHAPTER 1:
BUSINESS DEFINITION

1. What did you decide to paint on your store window? What does your NFP organization (or department) do, sell, provide, or produce?

2. What is your NFP's mission? Why does it exist? What purpose does it serve? Why are you in business?

3. Now write a simple mission statement for your NFP (or department).

4. In addition to your mission, what are some of the other capabilities of your NFP?

5. What are your organization's values and goals?

6. Describe the community environment in which your business functions; for example, what's the geography? Is it urban/rural? Is it highly competitive?

7. Describe the physical environment in which your business operates. For instance, is it or could it be free-standing? Does it function only within an institution? Is it centralized or does it have multiple sites?

8. Summarize the history of your business. Did it evolve over many years? Was it created to meet a need? How many times has it changed substantially?

9. How is your NFP organized? What are the structural definitions? How does it interface with other businesses in the institution? Draw the organization chart.

2

Products and Product Lines

PRODUCT LINE PROFITABILITY

Your business, as a whole, either makes or loses money. But it doesn't do it as a whole; it does it as a series of products or services, each one of which might make or lose money. For example, the Red Cross might have a positive bottom line; that is, it might make money overall. But it might make money on disaster service and lose money on the blood bank function.

Most organizations have a number of product lines, each with a different profitability. When all these lines are totaled, they determine the overall profitability of the company. It makes sense, then, that if you want to know about why a business does or doesn't make a profit, you would start by analyzing the components that make up the company's overall bottom line. Those components are products and product lines.

One of the first tasks you must undertake in optimizing your overall profitability is to determine what your products are, what your product lines are, and how much each of these products and product lines makes or loses for your business.

Not all products or product lines have to make a profit. Some organizations lose money on their most important products, but they know they have to make money in other ways to fund the losing line. This is an important concept.

Let's say that your business is a boys' and girls' club and that you get revenue from memberships, donations, whatever. You were chartered to provide counseling for underprivileged children from troubled families. There is no money in this, and your donations often fail to cover your costs. So you create a second product line that is more lucrative: summer day camps. The revenue from the camps is sufficient to cover the cost of the camps, plus extra to pay for the counseling. Your overall margin is positive.

It's okay to keep a losing line if it is important to your mission. But you must have a profitable line somewhere to make up the difference or your overall business will fail to sustain itself.

By breaking down a business into a set of product lines, each with its own products, you can analyze exactly where your company's profit (or lack thereof) is generated. You can then use that information to target corrective action to enhance your overall profitability.

At this point, you might be objecting to the word *product*. I recall a particularly animated conversation with a hospital executive who insisted that he didn't have "products," he had "services." Many NFP managers have the same discomfort with calling their services products. For the purposes of this book, they can be considered the same thing. However, it's harder to define a service, whereas you can more readily visualize a product sitting on a shelf and can see it in more concrete (and thus measurable) terms. For the exercises in this book, you may find it easier if you think of your services as products.

DETERMINING YOUR PRODUCTS

There is no magic rule about what makes a product or how products are clustered into product lines. As you examine your organization, you will want to look carefully at what you sell, because that will be your product(s). Then look for patterns that suggest how your products might cluster into product lines.

There are countless acceptable ways to define your products. You might find a natural order, or you might use a functional or academic order. Exhibit 2–1 gives some examples of the way products can be sorted.

A good way to start defining is by looking at how your payment comes. Since you will eventually want to compare reimbursement to costs to determine product profitability, you should make sure

Exhibit 2–1 Defining Your Products

	Hospital	*School*	*Museum*
By Activity	Heart Surgery Angioplasty Treadmill Tests	Math & Science Music & Arts Social Studies	General Public Private Tours Artist Receptions
By Function	Catering Meals Tray Line Meals Cafeteria Sales	Teaching Counseling Testing	Display Education Preservation
By Structure	Orthopedic Neurosurgery Cardiology	Elementary Middle High	Art Periods Individual Galleries Art Medium

that your products are defined in a fashion consistent with the payment mechanism. In fact, this is often a good place to start: look to see how your payment comes in.

If you still can't see a natural order for your products, try looking in a textbook on the subject and see how the table of contents structures the topics. Failing all else, you can make an arbitrary assignment.

The important thing is to divide your company's businesses into discrete segments that can each be measured without overlap or gaps. Your product definitions should be measurable (can I count them?), they should be discrete (no gaps or overlaps), and they should be logical (would this make sense to somebody else?).

ANALYZING PRODUCT PROFITABILITY

Our purpose here is to analyze products and product lines so that we can see which are contributing to profit and which are creating a loss. So we have to define each product succinctly enough that we can count its costs and its revenues, without overlap to other product costs or revenues. Therefore, it is critical that each identified product be defined in an objective and measurable way for data collection purposes.

For example, suppose you run a youth organization, and your product is summer swim camp. You need to be sure that you have an explicit definition of that customer category. In this case, you can use a code on your registration card that specifies this camper group. You can then sort all accounts by camp code, giving you data only on those campers whose primary interest was swim camp.

As you define your products, consider each one in light of how it is differentiated from other products in your business. Let's say you run a hospital dietary department. Are all meals counted together, or is there a way of sorting catering meals from patient trays from cafeteria line? In terms of payment, does it make sense to break meals down to this level, or do they all perform similarly?

Remember, the purpose is to target information so you can act on it. Be methodical and consistent in your approach. Avoid analysis to the point of paralysis, but do continue digging until you have a thorough understanding of the financial performance of every component of your business.

ACTING ON PRODUCT PROFITABILITY

Once you have identified your products and clustered them into product lines, you can collect data and calculate profit for each product and product line. Then you can use that information to help you make decisions about expanding or enhancing a service, or possibly cutting back on a service or eliminating it entirely. Even in a not-for-profit environment, the financial performance of a business function is an essential element to be considered in making business decisions.

QUESTIONS ON CHAPTER 2:
PRODUCTS AND PRODUCT LINES

1. What are your company's products? (What does it sell?)

2. How would you cluster your company's products into product lines? How many product lines might you have? Are there several different ways you might cluster your products to define your lines? What are the advantages/disadvantages of each option?

3. What method might you use to sort your products within each product line? Think about how your revenue is received. Does your proposed scheme account for each product in a discrete manner, ensuring that there is no overlap or omission?

4. How would you set about collecting data (volume, cost, reimbursement) on each of the products in each of your product lines?

5. If other people in your organization looked at your product line
   configuration, would they see the logic and order in it? How might you
   clarify it further?

3

Profit Formula

PROFIT ACCOUNTABILITY

Profit is an essential goal of all businesses, both for-profit and not-for-profit. NFPs should have excess revenue (profit) as their goal in order to support growth, expansion, and improved services, as well as to decrease dependence on outside sources of funding. Profits (excess revenue) can be used to offset future costs, improve quality of services, and help control citizen taxes. All businesses, including NFPs, should be required to generate sufficient revenue to cover their costs of operation; that is, they should be held accountable for achieving profitability. This concept is called profit accountability.

In Chapter 2 you identified the "products" that your NFP "sells." Now you must determine the profitability of each of those products as the first step in determining the overall profitability of your organization. To do that, you first must know what constitutes profit.

Suppose you run a research institute that is funded with government grants and private donations. At your current "burn rate," you're spending $100,000 more per month than you bring in. This means that you will exhaust all institute reserves within 18 months. Your board has told you quite explicitly to "fix it or else."

You know (and so does your board) that you are not profitable, but how do you know what to fix? What do you do? Where do you start? With the countless options in front of line managers, it's all but impossible to know which variables to manipulate to enhance profitability. Should you close down a lab? Fire the most senior technicians? Write more grant applications? Publish more impressive research results? Attend high-visibility conferences? Hire a Nobel Laureate? Sell interest in your institute to a private corporation? What would help? None of these? All of them? Or would that just make matters worse? The only way to know is to sort your options according to the mathematical formula that produces profit.

WHAT IS THE PROFIT FORMULA?

The profit formula simplifies all those variables into three elements: cost, revenue, and volume. That's all, just those three elements. Whenever you're faced with a profit concern, you have only to look at those three pieces to get a clear view of the issue at hand.

Profit is how much money you get for your product, minus how much it costs you to make and sell your product, multiplied by how many units of your product you sell. The following equation shows how they go together:

$$\text{Profit} = (\text{Revenue} - \text{Cost}) \times \text{Volume}$$

HOW THE PROFIT FORMULA WORKS

Imagine you run the Frozen Assets ice cream store, and want to know how much profit you make. First, calculate all the costs associated with a single unit of your product (one ice cream cone). This figure is called the unit cost (see Figure 3–1).

Figure 3–1 Unit Costs

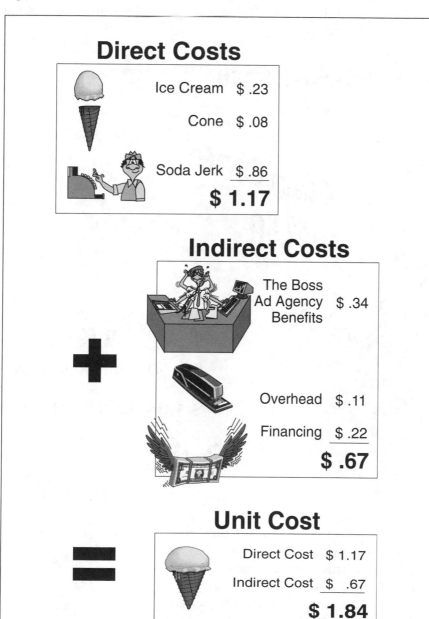

Direct Costs

Ice Cream	$ .23
Cone	$ .08
Soda Jerk	$ .86
	$ 1.17

Indirect Costs

The Boss Ad Agency Benefits	$ .34
Overhead	$ .11
Financing	$ .22
	$ .67

Unit Cost

Direct Cost	$ 1.17
Indirect Cost	$ .67
	$ 1.84

Next, figure out how much money you get for each cone. That will be your "unit revenue," or the amount of revenue you get for each unit of product.

Unit Revenue: $2.50

Unit Margin

$ 2.50	Unit Revenue
- $ 1.84	Unit Cost
$ .66	

Now you want to find out how much money you make (or lose) on each unit (each cone). This important piece of financial data is called the unit margin. To calculate the unit margin, subtract the per-cone cost from the per-cone revenue for a per-cone profit margin.

Once you have a unit margin, multiply that by volume to get total profit.

PROFIT

Unit Margin x Volume

APPLYING THE PROFIT FORMULA

Here's an example of how you can use the profit formula to target your analysis of a changing financial picture.

Center City Hospital is a not-for-profit community hospital that had always been a leader in the treatment of eye disease. Its patient services had been sorted into product lines (clusters of services) that included the eye center, orthopedics, cardiology, oncology, neurology, and several others. The eye center product line had historically provided more than 50 percent of the hospital's operating gain (Figure 3–2A). This particular year, the eye center reported a $1.5 million profit. This made the chief executive officer very happy, until somebody pointed out that despite this very large profit, the eye center had actually made $1 million less this year than it did last year.

To find out why, the managers analyzed the data using the profit formula (Figure 3–2B). They compared each of the three profit variables to those of last year, before the dramatic drop, and they found the following:

- Volume of service was up 42 percent.
- Revenue (per unit) was up 5.4 percent.
- Cost (per unit) was up 11.9 percent.

Since the volume was up, the loss couldn't be due to volume, and since the revenue was up too, that wasn't the problem either. By eliminating those two variables, they concluded that the change had to be the result of increased costs.

The 29 percent drop in unit margin was the root cause of the loss—the eye center had gone from making money on each patient to losing money on each patient. With a loss on every sale, the increased volume of service compounded the loss, creating the enormous hit to the bottom line.

Once the managers knew it was a cost problem, they examined each of the products in the eye center product line, again comparing this year to last (Figure 3–2C). They looked at changes in profitability for glaucoma, infections, cataracts, hyphema, trauma, and others.

Sorting the financial data this way was very revealing. One product, cataracts, had shown a dramatic drop in profit margin that was

Figure 3–2 Eye Center Profitability Analysis

A) Hospital Product Lines

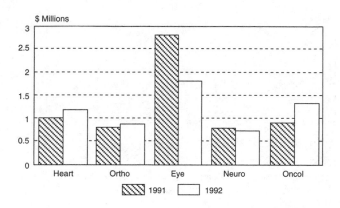

B) Eye Center Profits

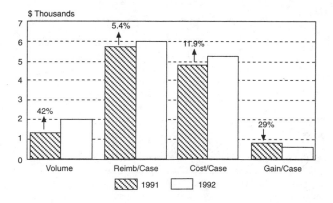

Figure 3–2 continued

C) Eye Center Products

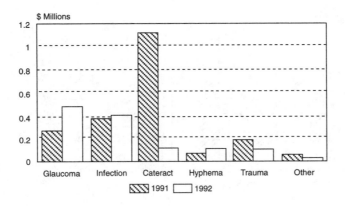

D) Costs by Department

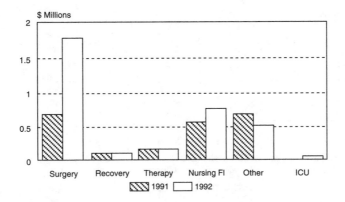

roughly equal to that of the parent product line, which seemed to account for the overall deficiency. Since the managers had already demonstrated that the change was cost-related, they knew they needed only to analyze the cost of cataracts to locate the source of the decline.

The cost allocation by department (Figure 3–2D) showed a $1 million increase in costs within the operating room, so the managers met with the operating room staff to look for possible explanations. The clinicians were quick to suggest that the new laser procedure they had installed last year was the culprit. Armed with that information, the managers were able to establish operational and pricing guidelines to minimize this deficit. They set policies for use of the expensive equipment, and raised the price to patients on whom the expensive equipment was used. Concurrently, they promoted the glaucoma service, which had performed very favorably during the same time period. Increased marketing of this service increased the volume, and thus improved overall profits.

Without the detailed financial information provided by a product profitability analysis, the $1 million loss would have been a vague and unmanageable event, putting the eye center at risk of insolvency. The managers were able to recognize the $1.5 million "good profit" for what it was, a large red flag warning of a major financial change in a lucrative service, a downward trend that would undoubtedly dip into red ink before the next year's reports were issued.

As you research the facts underlying your financial reports, keep in mind this bit of wisdom from Celia Green: "The way to do research is to attack the facts at the point of greatest astonishment." When you examine a financial profile, find the biggest deviation and track it down. Methodically analyze each of the profit variables and compare it to previous performance to explain the present and anticipate the future.

REPORTING PROFIT VARIABLES

The most common mechanism for reporting the three profit variables is the financial spreadsheet. This is a fairly standard format that becomes more friendly as you learn the accountants' lingo for cost, revenue, and volume.

Take a look at the sample spreadsheet in Exhibit 3–1 as you go over the new terms defined in Exhibit 3–2. Take the time to find each term on the spreadsheet, and play with the numbers a while until you see how they relate to each other.

JUST A NOTE ON DATA

In NFP organizations, where profitability has not historically been a mandate, many managers have developed the habit of (1) ignoring data, (2) denying data, (3) blaming data, (4) saying there are no data, or (5) all of the above. Particularly when data are not encouraging, it is tempting to fault the data, rather than assuming (reasonable) accuracy and doing something about it.

Your profitability management efforts should be guided by financial data and your analysis , which suggests that you will undoubtedly encounter some or all of the obstacles above, either in your own mind or in the minds of those around you. It can be disconcerting to face inexact or incomplete information, and of course you must make every effort to ensure accuracy and completeness. However, it is very rare that you will ever refine the figures to perfection. At some point you just have to trust the data and act on them, because they're the best you're going to get, and they're better than nothing.

In 1952, CBS rented the new Univac computer to provide election results. But when the computer projected that Dwight Eisenhower would swamp Adlai Stevenson, the network had Charles Collingwood report that the computer couldn't make up its mind. Because the executives didn't trust the data, CBS missed scooping one of the biggest political landslides in history.

ANALYZING PRODUCT PROFIT

Your goal is to determine the profitability of each of your products, and then manage the factors that affect that variable in order to improve product profitability. If you do this with each of your products and each of your product lines, your overall profitability will improve.

Exhibit 3–1 Typical P&L Spreadsheet

Patient Admissions by Insurance Group

	Patient Volume	Gross Revenue	Net Revenue	Revenue Percent	Variable Cost	Contribution Margin	Fixed Cost	Total Cost	Cost Percent	Operating Gain/Loss	Margin
MEDICARE	143	136,372	77,281	56.67	47,566	29,715	66,545	114,111	83.68	(36,830)	–47.66
HMO/PPO	47	23,931	18,924	79.08	12,118	6,806	13,681	25,799	107.81	(6,875)	–36.33
MILITARY	3	3,304	2,938	88.91	748	2,190	1,033	1,781	53.89	1,157	39.38
COMMERCIAL	22	10,690	9,140	85.80	6,470	2,670	8,334	14,804	138.48	(5,664)	–61.97
WORKER'S COMP	2	155	133	85.81	213	(80)	378	591	381.46	(458)	–344.54
UNINSURED	63	10,003	5,249	52.48	9,292	(4,043)	13,888	23,180	231.73	(17,931)	–341.60
TOTAL	280	184,455	113,665	61.62	76,407	37,258	103,859	180,266	97.73	(66,601)	–58.59
PER PATIENT	N/A	659	406	0.22	273	133	371	644	97.73	(238)	–58.59

Exhibit 3–2 Spreadsheet Definitions

Contribution Margin—The amount of revenue left over after the variable cost is covered; this is the amount that "contributes" toward the fixed costs of the institution. Calculated by subtracting the Variable Cost from the Net Revenue.

Cost Percent—The Total Cost expressed as a percent of the Gross Revenue. Calculated by dividing the Total Cost by the Gross Revenue, then multiplying by 100 (to make it a percent).

Fixed Cost—That component of the total cost that you incur regardless of the volume of business you do.

Gross Revenue—The total dollars billed. This figure represents charges, not receipts or costs.

Margin—The profit expressed as a ratio of surplus to Net Revenue. Calculated by dividing the Operating Gain by the Net Revenue, then multiplying it by 100 (to make it a percent).

Net Revenue—Total dollars received from all sources.

Operating Gain/Loss—The surplus (or deficit) remaining after all costs have been deducted from all revenue. Also known as PROFIT (or LOSS). Calculated by subtracting the Total Cost from the Net Revenue.

Revenue Percent—This is how much you collect on the dollar. A Revenue Percent of 52.49 means you collected 52.49 cents for every dollar billed. It is calculated by first dividing the total dollars received by the total dollars billed, times 100 (to make it a percent), which gives you a Deductions Percent, or how much is written off from the amount billed (how much you didn't collect). You then subtract that figure from 100 to get the Revenue Percent. The Deductions Percent is the flip side of the Revenue Percent.

Total Cost—This represents all costs of any kind applied to the account. Calculated by adding the Variable Cost and the Fixed Cost.

Variable Cost—That component of the total cost that varies with volume. The Variable Cost and Fixed Cost together make the Total Cost.

Volume—The number of units being measured.

To do this, you will first need to measure the cost, revenue, and volume for your products. Then you can examine the many factors that contribute to or influence each variable. Start by completing a Profitability Worksheet (Exhibit 3–3) for each of your products. When you're through, enter the summary data from each Profitability Worksheet into a Product Line Analysis, as shown in Exhibit 3–4.

Presenting the data in this methodical format will allow you to visualize the whole picture at once, enabling you to pinpoint areas of concern and target actions for improvement.

Now look at Exhibit 3–5. This shows which accounting data measure these three elements, and also which variables you can manipulate to enhance profitability.

The next few chapters provide greater detail for ways to measure cost, revenue, and volume, as well as ways to enhance financial performance in each of these three areas.

Exhibit 3–3 Profitability Worksheet

(Complete One Form for Each Product)

Product Description: _____

_____

UNIT COST

DIRECT COSTS		INDIRECT COSTS	
Labor	_____	Labor	_____
Supplies	_____	Overhead	_____
Equipment	_____		_____
Facilities	_____		_____
	_____		_____

TOTAL DIRECT: _____   TOTAL INDIRECT: _____

TOTAL COST PER UNIT: _____

CHARGE/PRICE		UNIT REVENUE	
Break-Even	_____	High	_____
This Organization	_____	Low	_____
Industry Standard	_____	Average	_____
Competitors:	_____		

UNIT MARGIN		VOLUME PER YEAR	
Unit Cost	_____	Previous Year	_____
Unit Revenue	_____	Current Year	_____
Unit Margin	_____	Next Year Expected	_____

PRODUCT IMPORTANCE

Other Considerations:

Gross Revenues per Year	_____	_____
New Revenues per Year	_____	_____
Percent of Profit	_____	_____

Exhibit 3–4 Product Line Analysis

PRODUCT	Frozen Assets Ice Cream Store					
	Annual Volume	% of Volume	Unit Cost	Unit Revenue	Unit Margin	Profit/ (Loss)
Regular	12,600	70	$1.84	$2.27	$0.43	$5,418
Senior	3,600	20	$1.84	$1.93	$0.09	$324
Gourmet	1,620	9	$2.09	$4.02	$1.93	$3,127
Slugs ("Friends")	180	1	$1.84	$0.00	($1.84)	($331)
AVERAGE:	18,000	100	$1.86	$2.34	$0.47	$8,537

Exhibit 3–5 Measuring and Manipulating Profit

	To **Measure** Profit Monitor These Parameters	To **Manipulate** Profit Change These Parameters
Cost	Fixed Cost Variable Cost Cost Percent	Productivity Staffing Mix Operating Protocols Standing Orders Operating Procedures Supplies Equipment Maintenance Leases Service Intensity Overhead
Revenue	Revenue Percent Payer Mix	Pricing Billing Accounts Receivable Collections Write-Offs Lost Charges
Volume	Annual Volume Volume Trends	Customer Service Customer Behaviors Competition Pricing Repeat Business Marketing Advertising Distribution/Access

QUESTIONS ON CHAPTER 3: PROFIT FORMULA

1. What is meant by the term *profit accountability?* How does this apply to an NFP? Why would an NFP want to make a profit?

2. What is the profit formula? What are the three components (profit variables)? How do they relate to each other to produce profit?

3. Explain unit cost. How is it calculated? What does it tell you?

4. Explain unit revenue. How is it calculated? What does it tell you?

5. What is a unit margin? How is it calculated? What does it tell you?

6. What is a spreadsheet? What does it tell you?

7. Now, complete a Profitability Worksheet (Exhibit 3–3) for each of your NFP's products (as you defined them in Chapter 2). You'll need to make enough copies of the worksheet so that you can have one for each of your products/ services. This should take some time, so you may want to work on it off and on for a couple of days.

8. Once you've finished the Profitability Worksheets for each of your products, complete a Product Line Analysis (Exhibit 3–4) for the products in your NFP.

⚜
4

Minimizing Costs

FIGURING OUT COSTS

The other day my 10-year-old son asked for my help with a school sale. His team was selling candy (what else?), and he had gone to Toys-Я-Us with his grandfather and purchased a large bag of individually wrapped candies. He eagerly told me his plan. He was going to put the candy in little bags with a couple of baseball cards and sell each bag for $5.00.

I pointed out that the first step was to determine how much each piece cost so that he would know how much he had to sell it for to break even. Then he would know how low he could set the price to undercut his competition.

Together we counted the individual pieces (all 150 of them), and divided that number into the package price of $7.00 to get a cost-per-unit price of 4.6¢.

"Wow, we could sell them for a nickel each!" he exclaimed.

"Yeah, but what about your other costs," I asked, "like your time, and Grandpa's time?"

"Whatdaya mean, my time? And besides, Grandpa wasn't doing anything anyway," he responded.

"And how about the gas to go to the store, and the baggies to package the candy in, and whose baseball cards are you using, and . . ."

He interrupted with, "They're not keepers, Mom, they're Gabe's old ones. They're not worth anything."

To make a long story short, Kellen eventually settled on 50¢ per bag, which reduced the cost enough to encourage sales volume, and he made a nice profit of $23.00 on the day for the school.

The purpose of this story is to illustrate the complexity of cost allocation. To determine profit, you must first have a comprehensive understanding of all the costs you incurred in creating and selling your product. Cost accounting is the accurate expression for calculating and allocating costs. For our purposes, we can consider it "cost figuring-out."

COST VOCABULARY

There are a lot of ways to categorize costs, which contributes to the confusion around accounting terms. For instance, all costs can be considered either fixed or variable. Or costs can be divided into salary and nonsalary. A very common grouping is Direct, Indirect, Overhead, and Capital costs.

	Direct	Indirect	Overhead	Capital
Salary	Fixed Variable	Fixed Variable	Fixed Variable	100% Fixed
Nonsalary	Fixed Variable	Fixed Variable	Fixed Variable	100% Fixed

Fixed vs. Variable Costs

A fixed cost is one you have regardless of volume, whereas a variable cost increases as volume increases. Consider a commercial airliner going from San Diego to Boston. What expenses would be incurred even if there were no passengers?

The plane itself and the pilots are essential, as well as gas, and there might be a requirement for a minimum complement of cabin attendants. These are fixed costs.

Now let's add passengers. As the volume of passengers increases, certain costs increase. These include food and drinks, more flight attendants, and maybe a little more gas to accommodate the increased weight of the extra people and baggage. These are the variable costs, since they vary with volume (see Figure 4–1).

Fixed costs remain constant regardless of volume, while variable costs fluctuate as volume changes.

Salary vs. Nonsalary Costs

This self-explanatory grouping simply sorts labor costs from all other costs. This can be particularly revealing in organizations with heavy labor intensity.

Figure 4–1 Fixed Costs vs. Variable Costs.

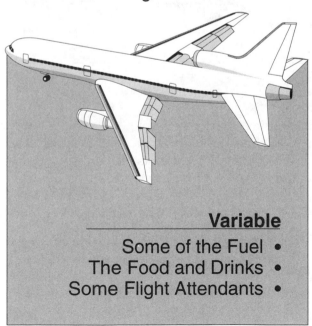

Fixed

- The Airplane
- Most of the Fuel
- The Pilots
- Most of the Flight Attendants

Variable

Some of the Fuel •
The Food and Drinks •
Some Flight Attendants •

Figure 4–2 Direct Costs

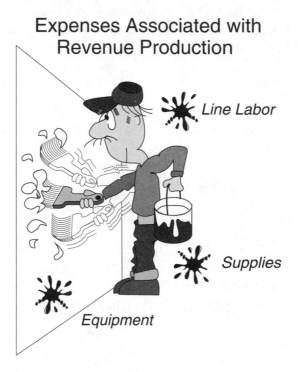

Expenses Associated with Revenue Production

Line Labor

Supplies

Equipment

Direct Costs

We think of direct costs as those being associated directly with revenue production—those things needed to make or sell the product. You'll usually find direct costs on departmental budgets. Examples would be salaries for the labor force on the production line or at the sales counter, or equipment and supplies used by those people. Direct costs can be both fixed and variable, and both salary and nonsalary (see Figure 4–2).

Indirect Costs

Indirect costs are close to, but not at, the point of service. For example, in schools, indirect costs may be administrative support, record keeping, and building maintenance. In city government it

Figure 4–3 Indirect Costs

- Both Fixed and Variable
- Highly Volume-Sensitive
- Close to the Point of Service
- Examples:
    - *Admitting*
    - *Dietary*
    - *Records*
    - *Housekeeping*

might be billing for utility services, fleet maintenance, or ordinance management. In a hospital the indirect departments would be admitting, dietary, medical records, or housekeeping (see Figure 4–3).

While indirect costs can be both fixed and variable, they are usually very volume-sensitive. This makes sense. The higher the student enrollment, the more classrooms to be maintained, records to be kept, and people needed to keep them. These costs will be both salary and nonsalary.

Overhead Costs

Those functions that do not generate revenue but do contribute to the overall functioning of the business are considered overhead. Overhead includes services such as telephones, rent, lights, electricity, utilities, maintenance, and landscaping. Examples of overhead departments include administration, accounting, and marketing (see Figure 4–4).

They will have salary and nonsalary categories, and can be both fixed and variable. They are usually not volume-sensitive, since

---

Figure 4–4 Overhead

- Both Fixed & Variable
- Non-Revenue-Producing
- Not Volume-Sensitive

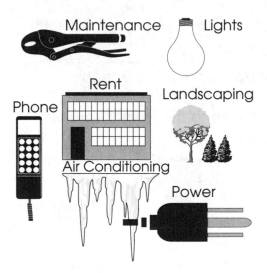

- Examples of Overhead Departments
    - *Administration*
    - *Accounting*
    - *Facilities*
    - *Marketing*

employees of these departments usually don't flex with business volume.

Capital Costs

Unlike Direct, Indirect, and Overhead costs, the cost of Capital is always fixed, never variable. That's because Capital costs refer to the financial expenses of depreciation on equipment, insurance debt, and interest on loans (see Figure 4–5).

Capital can be categorized as Assignable, meaning that it is area-specific, or Unassignable, in which case it is distributed by a general formula such as square footage.

Figure 4–5 Capital Costs

- Examples:
  - *depreciation*
  - *insurance*
  - *interest*

- Assignable *(area-specific)*

- Unassignable *(square footage)*

COST DETAIL

Cost accounting reports vary widely from one institution to another. As you look at the internal cost reports for your organization, you should be able to locate the generic categories described above.

Figure 4–6 is an example of cost detail featuring the cost of Kellogg's Corn Flakes that was published in the November 1992 *Consumer Reports* magazine .

Figure 4–6 Cost Detail Example

Corn Flakes	
Raw Material	$ .14
Processing	$ .26
Labor	$ .06
Freight	$ .08
Packaging	$ .12
Advertising	$ .21
Marketing/Sales	$ .55
Wholesale to Store	**$1.73**
Retail to Consumer	**$2.20**

Source: "Why Does Cereal Cost So Much?" Copyright 1992 by Consumers Union of U.S., Inc., Yonkers, NY 10703-1057. Reprinted by permission from CONSUMER REPORTS, November 1992.

Figure 4–7 University Mail Service.

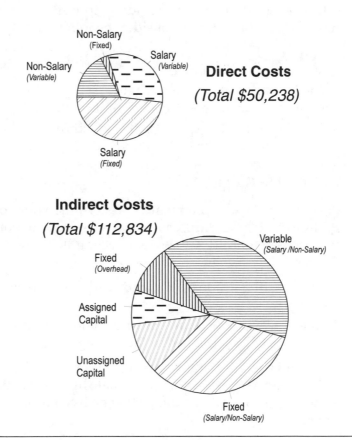

Figure 4–7 shows the cost detail for an NFP mail service. Notice how each of the groupings relates to the others.

COST MEASURES

Now that you know what the terminology means and how it is presented in a cost report, you should consider which of those variables to measure in order to monitor your costs and ultimately, of course, your profits. If you have the luxury of a computerized cost accounting system, you will have more things to monitor than any human being should be allowed to have. But if you have to do the calculations by hand, you will need to prioritize your time around a few key categories that can provide you most of the information you will need. For instance, consider the following:

- **Cost per Unit:** What is the true cost of producing and selling each individual product?
- **Total Cost:** What is the aggregate cost of producing and selling all products combined (cost per unit multiplied by volume)?
- **Cost Percent:** What is the Total Cost expressed as a percentage of the company's Gross Revenue?

CALCULATING COST

The data you need to tabulate to determine your costs are outlined in Exhibit 4–1. Once you know what information you need, you must methodically set about collecting it. There are two ways to do this:

1. prospectively (looking ahead to determine the theoretical costs) or
2. retrospectively (looking historically to determine your actual costs, usually presented in the aggregate)

My friend George wants to run a taco stand on the beach in Baja California. Let's say you want to calculate his cost per unit. First, do it prospectively. List all the things that go into one taco. Include the following:

- For direct costs, you will need to examine salary costs (the cook) and nonsalary costs (lettuce, cheese, etc.).
- For indirect costs, you also will need to examine salary costs (cashier) and nonsalary costs (beach chairs).
- Then there's overhead. Again, you must examine salary costs (the local lawyer) and nonsalary costs (rent on the hut).
- Finally, you will need to examine capital costs, such as equipment (the deep fryer), insurance costs (liability, medical), and interest (the Small Business Administration loan).

Next, figure out a reasonable amount to allocate to each item. For example, what's the cook's hourly rate, and how many tacos does

Exhibit 4–1 Calculating Costs

Direct Costs

   Salary: _____

   Supplies: _____

   Equipment: _____

   Facilities: _____

   Other: _____

   Total Direct Costs | |

Indirect Costs | |

Overhead | |

Capital | |

Total Cost | |

---

the cook turn out in the average hour? How many tortillas come in a package, and how much does the package cost?

Add up all these figures, and you should have a reasonable prospective estimate of the cost of producing one taco. Now you can multiply that by the number of tacos George will sell in a year, and you'll have the Total Cost. Divide that by the Gross Revenues (the total amount of money George can expect to collect), and you'll have his Cost Percent.

The weak link here is that this estimate relies on a prospective calculation, which is a theoretical figure. Its value depends on your accuracy in assigning costs and projecting volumes. If George's cook is too generous with the cheese, you'll overshoot your mark.

A more accurate method is a retrospective analysis of actual costs over the preceding year or so. The process is much the same, except that you pull the invoices and find out what was actually paid, and then divide that by the volume actually produced.

A great example of a prospective budget is one constructed for a grant application. You list all the things for which you think you'll need money to do the project you propose, and then you add the costs of all items so that you can tell the agency how much money you want it to give you.

A retrospective budget is one the finance department constructs for a department based on its records of the department's past performance. Retrospective costs tend to be depressing, while prospective cost projections run the risk of being optimistic bordering on fantasy.

It is very common for new businesses to create a prospective budget, then switch to a retrospective system after they have a little experience. A new consumer advocacy agency may have to estimate income and expenses for the first year or two. But once a clear record of expenditures and revenue has been collected, the retrospective data can be used to project costs more accurately.

INFLUENCING COST

What do you do once you know what your true costs are, especially if they're too high? One way to increase profitability is to reduce costs, so your goal must be to influence variables that affect cost. There are many ways to do this. In the taco stand example, you might have George consider the following:

- **Productivity:** Can you create an incentive for your cook to increase the number of tacos produced each hour?
- **Staffing:** Can the cook also take the money, thereby eliminating the need for a cashier? Did you need to hire a French gourmet, or could the local cantina cook do the job? Do you need a complete housekeeping service, or can the cook sweep the floor before going home?
- **Supplies:** Can each patron be handed a single napkin, rather than leaving the dispenser on the table where the napkins can be grabbed by handfuls?

- **Standing Orders:** Is there a reason you routinely put guacamole on the side, or is it just a garnish you used to be able to afford and never questioned?
- **Equipment:** If you replace your 25-year-old deep fryer with a new version that uses half the oil, will it save you money in the long run?
- **Maintenance:** Is there any way to get out of that costly maintenance agreement you signed when you bought the cash register? Can you consolidate all your maintenance needs under a single deal with the mechanic across the road?
- **Leases:** Is it cheaper to rent the hut, or should you buy it outright? Are you fully using all the space you have? Are there expensive "extras" included in the lease that might be negotiated more favorably?
- **Overhead:** Last but not least, "overhead" is where a lot of the intangible costs end up. Consider inventory control, for instance. Have you noticed the cook nibbling at your cheese all day? What about that Yellow Pages ad; did it really increase your volume enough to cover the cost? This is the hardest area to quantify, and often the largest cost component.

CONCLUSION

Together, cost and revenue make up the unit profit margin. More often than not, cost is the one you are best able to influence, and therefore it is more important to you. Once you've set up cost monitors and gotten costs under control, you're ready to look at the next variable in the profit formula: revenues. Chapter 5 addresses revenue enhancement.

QUESTIONS ON CHAPTER 4: MINIMIZING COSTS

1. What's the difference between fixed and variable costs?

2. What is meant by salary or nonsalary sorting?

3. Define each of these cost accounting terms:
   - Direct Costs

   - Indirect Costs

   - Overhead

   - Capital

4. How would you calculate a prospective cost per unit for one of your NFP's products? How would you calculate a retrospective cost per unit for the same product?

5. How would you determine Total Cost and Cost Percent?

6. How would you influence cost in each of the following cost variables:

- Productivity

- Staffing

- Standing Orders/Policies

- Supplies

- Equipment

- Maintenance

- Leases

- Overhead

---- 🐚 ----

5

Maximizing Revenues

TERMINOLOGY

"Revenue" is what we actually get paid for the product or service we provide. Revenue is different from "cost." Cost is what the business pays out of pocket in order to produce the product. And don't confuse revenue with the "charge," or the "price"; that's the amount you ask for on the sticker. Revenue is the money that actually crosses your palm, and it can be completely unrelated to either cost or charge.

Let's go back to the ice cream cones discussed in Chapter 3. Each one costs you $1.84 to produce, and the sign on your counter says they sell for $2.50 each. But you might make a special deal for someone who buys several, or you might discount that unpopular flavor, or inflate the price of the most popular brand. And you might have a special friend who drops by every once in a while for a free cone. At the end of the day, you determine that you made 52 cones and have $118.04 in the cash drawer. So your total revenue was $118.04 for the day, for an average revenue of $2.27 per cone.

Revenue Terminology	
Cost:	$1.84
Price:	2.50
Revenue:	2.27

As Ross Perot would say, "Simple stuff, right?" You know your average revenue is $2.27, regardless of your costs or your price. (Are you ready yet to tackle the national debt?)

REVENUE IN A NOT-FOR-PROFIT WORLD

In a not-for-profit world, the revenue can come as a form of sale, such as a check for membership. But it also can come in a lump sum as a subsidy of sorts. For example, the post office gets revenue from the sale of stamps, but it also gets revenue budgeted to it from tax dollars. The city zoo gets revenue from a wide variety of "sales" sources: admissions at the gate, group activity sales, sales of its animals to other zoos, annual memberships in the zoological society, tuition to its Animal Friends classes, sales in its restaurants and curio shops, and internal sales to the bus tour and children's petting zoo. On top of these sales revenues, the zoo also gets very substantial revenue from philanthropic sources, and it has some limited revenue from grants for research in animal husbandry. All of these revenue sources provide the "cash" the zoo needs to pay its bills.

MEASURES OF REIMBURSEMENT

Where do you look on a financial spreadsheet to find out about your revenue? Several important data points are included on a standard spreadsheet, and you should be familiar with each.

- **Gross Revenue:** Gross revenue refers to the total amount billed. This figure reflects the charge, not the amount actually received.
- **Total Net Revenue:** Total net revenue is the total amount of money collected from all sources.
- **Net Revenue per Unit:** If the total net revenue is divided by the total number of product units sold, the resulting figure is the net revenue per unit.
- **Revenue Percent:** The revenue percent is the money collected compared to the amount billed. This is the "cents on the dollar." The flip side of this is the Deductions Percent, which is how much you lose, or write off, on the dollar.

PAYER CATEGORIES

Most businesses can group their customers into several categories based on the average price each group pays. For example, let's say the Frozen Assets ice cream shop offers a seniors' discount. Your seniors pay an average of $1.93 per cone, not the $2.27 of your regular customers. You need to know this, and you need to know what percentage of your business comes from seniors so that you know the total impact your discount has on your overall revenue.

In health care, the payer categories have become incredibly complex. These categories include Medicare, Medicaid, workers' compensation, commercial/indemnity insurance, managed care (health maintenance organization/preferred provider organization [HMO/PPO]), various local government programs, and the uninsured or self-paid. Each of these payer groups has a different payment scheme with a different average revenue to the provider. Table 5–1 shows how widely payers vary in the amount they pay on each dollar billed.

Table 5–1 Variability in Amount Paid on Each Dollar Billed

Payer	Cents on the Dollar	
	Inpatient	Outpatient
Medicare	.55	.47
Medicaid	.31	.26
HMO/PPO	.57	.77
County Aid	.22	.25
Military	.72	.89
Commercial	.96	.87
Workers' Compensation	.99	.86

REVENUE TYPES

In health care, the revenue is called "reimbursement," because that's how it actually occurs. The hospital provides the care, bills the payer, and is reimbursed based on the particular payment contract of that payer. The health care arena makes a good example for communicating revenue concepts, because just about every conceivable formula can be found in play in health care right now.

For example, take the concept of charge-based versus cost-based reimbursement. This simply asks, does Blue Cross reimburse the hospital based on what the hospital bill asks (charge based), or on what Blue Cross thinks it should reasonably have cost the hospital to deliver the service (cost based)? Big difference.

What about fee-for-service versus fixed fee? The best example of this is the difference between ordering off the menu at McDonald's® or just taking the kids' meal package. If you go into the hospital you'll get a bill that itemizes dozens of little supplies and services you don't understand and probably would rather not hear about. You just care about that number at the end—you know, the one with all the zeros after it. That's an example of fee for service.

But when the total gets too high, the payers begin challenging it. As in the earlier example, they begin looking for alternatives. In this case, they came up with a package price based on what they think a similar illness would cost in a similar circumstance. They give the hospital that fixed fee, regardless of what services were actually delivered or what it cost the hospital for the care of that patient. That's fixed fee.

It's important that you know each of your payer types, the average revenue for each, and the percentage of each payer type for your particular payer mix. These variables will help you control revenue and adjust your pricing in response to changing market dynamics. Figures 5–1 and 5–2 show you some ways to look at your payer mix.

INFLUENCING REVENUE

Is revenue fixed in stone, or are there ways to enhance it? Is there a way to push the $2.27 per cone a little closer to $2.50 or even beyond? Well, there are several variables that affect revenue, so there should be at least that many opportunities to enhance it.

Before the Sale

Pricing

Unless you are in a fixed-fee environment, the price you set is the greatest single determinant of your ultimate total revenue. Pricing itself is an extremely complex strategy that is the subject of many

Figure 5–1 Payer Financial Information, Frozen Assets Ice Cream Store

A) Operating Gain
Annual Profits

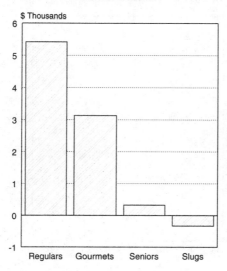

B) Unit Margin
Average Profit per Cone

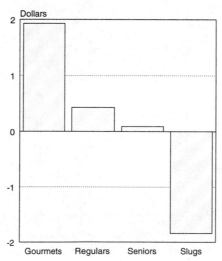

Figure 5–1 continued

C) Volume

Annual Sales Volume

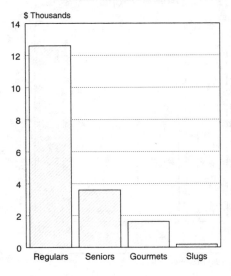

D) Cost

Average Cost per Cone

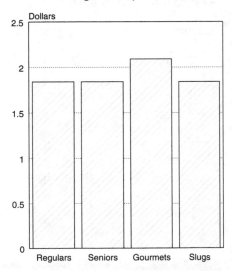

Figure 5–2 Payer Mix Profile

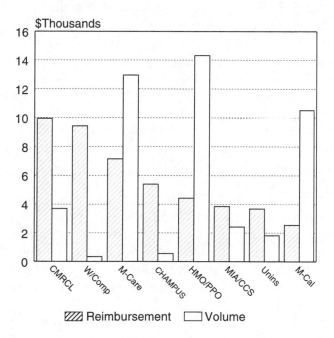

volumes of text. There are lots of ways to set price. The goal, of course, is to cover your costs, and many prices are merely a function of a "cost-plus" markup. You cover your costs, plus a little extra for your efforts. This is a common pricing strategy in retail businesses. For example, look at car dealerships. They take their factory sticker price, hike it up by a mystery number, then sell it to the consumer.

The cost-plus markup works well as long as the price remains reasonable in the eyes of the buyer. When it becomes unreasonable, as happened in health care, the payers begin to question the price, and they start looking for ways to change the reimbursement (revenue) formula.

Another pricing strategy is "what the market will bear." This means pricing as high as possible without turning away the customer. My father recently told me that the problem with the world today (sounds like a father, doesn't it?) is that most vendors set prices as high as they think they can get, whereas in his day they were kept to a fair profit.

A very critical component in pricing is competition. You have to watch what the other guy is charging and remain price-competitive, or else have some other powerful way to differentiate yourself.

Keep in mind that pricing is nearly worthless if you are not playing in an open market. In health care today, for example, the price can be the least important variable to consider, since the big payers (Medicare, Medicaid, and the big insurance companies) have sufficient power to ignore what you ask for and just pay you what they think you deserve. So the price on your invoice is often a waste of your time, since the revenue is predetermined by the payers with little input from you.

Payer Mix

Once you have a profile of your payer mix, you can begin working to improve it. For example, if your seniors are carrying too big a share of your ice cream market, consider adding an elite group by offering and advertising gourmet gelatto at a higher price. Or consider eliminating that small but recurring group of nonpaying friends.

If your not-for-profit business serves mainly the economically disadvantaged, consider adding upper-income levels to your users by offering products or services that would appeal to them. Or perhaps you could expand your services into other neighborhoods. If you've catered only to local citizens, you might expand your service region to broaden your payer mix. Just remember, the goal is to increase your average revenue per sale, so you should be expanding in the direction of higher payers to offset your less lucrative customers.

Contracting

Make a deal with the retirement home to deliver ice cream cones every Tuesday at a special rate. You'll drop your price a little, but increase volume to accommodate the smaller margin. Schools can contract with local businesses to provide after-hours training for corporate employees. A not-for-profit alcohol abuse agency could contract with local legal and judicial systems for referrals.

Contracts can be a very powerful way to increase your profit, but they're only as good as the deal you negotiate. To make a viable contract, you must first have solid financial data about your business and your margins. If your quote is less than your costs, the added volume will only dig your hole deeper.

During the Sale

Qualification/Preapproval

This has tremendous application for businesses with eligibility requirements, such as memberships or authorizations. For example, health care insurers often require preauthorization before service is rendered. The concept here is to minimize delivery of products or services to someone who will not be able to pay. When you call for auto club roadside service, the tow-truck operator always asks to see your card before hooking up your car. Even when there is no formal prerequisite, a wise business owner makes some assumptions about the customer's likelihood of paying, and if in doubt, asks to see the cash before delivering the goods.

Not-for-profits often have sliding fee schedules to accommodate poor and indigent populations. The YWCA/YMCA and many other youth camps have two rates, one for members and a higher one for nonmembers. Each of these groups could really jeopardize their revenue unless they pay close attention to the rate that is authorized for each payer.

Documentation/Coding/Charging

Many businesses are paid some time after services are rendered. For example, a temporary agency provides a typist and bills the client for the hours worked. The process of documenting and/or coding services delivered becomes the mechanism for subsequent payment. The agency is at risk for lost revenue unless the system of documenting that service is efficient and accurate. Especially in

Revenue Variables

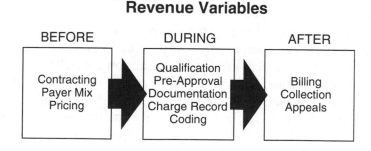

BEFORE	DURING	AFTER
Contracting Payer Mix Pricing	Qualification Pre-Approval Documentation Charge Record Coding	Billing Collection Appeals

large bureaucratic systems, the potential exists to enhance revenue enormously by improving accuracy of documentation systems.

The public schools in our neighborhood understand this concept very well. They know they get money from the district according to their "average daily attendance," or ADA. The ADA includes students who are home sick, but not those who just don't show up. To optimize their ADA, the schools ask you to call them if your child is sick; when you forget, they're quick to call you so that they get the best ADA payment they can.

After the Sale

Billing

A while back, my nephew Corey came to our hospital emergency room with his father to get a few stitches. The doctor explained the billing process to Corey's father: "Don't worry, you won't get a bill for this because you have money. The only people who get bills from our hospital are those who don't have money. The ones with money or insurance never seem to make it into the system." This exchange is true; I heard it myself. And it occurred in a hospital I was working with at the time. It was really embarrassing to hear one of our doctors say that to a patient (especially one of my relatives).

Unfortunately, he wasn't very far from the truth. The billing system at that particular institution was archaic and incredibly inefficient. The best way for the hospital to increase its revenue would be to focus on improving the system by which bills are generated. Of course, if you've been paying attention, you'll quickly point out that many health care payers don't regard the bill anyway, so maybe it doesn't matter after all. But there's a big difference between saving money by electing not to bill, and billing inefficiently and thereby losing money.

The most efficient billing system I know of is that of American Express. When you combine the American Express system with that of Nordstrom, which is a close second, you get lightning-speed billing. I once charged a purchase at Nordstrom on Monday and received the bill in the mail from American Express on the following Thursday. No lie! This is a wonderful benchmark for your not-

for-profit. I guarantee that if you are able to match this performance, it will do wonders for your profitability.

Collection/Appeals

Assuming that your bills did make it out to the customer, you can
further enhance revenues by increasing the amount you collect on
each dollar billed. Sometimes there are disputes, or occasionally a
bad debt. But many, many times customers just need someone to
nag them into paying. You should have a good sense of the cost of
this collection effort against the return you get for it. For example, a
small community clinic was closing down and was left with about
50 outstanding accounts. The clinic decided to retain the billing
clerk (at a rate of $12 per hour) for another two months to be sure all
the collections were made. On the surface, this seemed reasonable,
since it would take a couple of months to get the money in, even if
people were quick to respond. However, under closer scrutiny it
didn't make sense at all.

The cost of this effort would be $4,100 in salary, plus $1,250 in
benefits, for a total labor cost of $5,350. Clinic records showed that
the average bill was $63, so the entire outstanding debt was only
about $3,150. With an industry collection rate of 50 percent, the
clinic was likely to collect only $1,575. It made no sense to spend
$5,350 to collect $1,575. Collection companies are in business because it often is too costly for an organization to attempt its own
collections.

UNIT PROFITABILITY

After you have optimized the revenue for your product, you can
measure that against the cost of production to determine the profit
margin on each unit of product, that is, the profit on each ice cream
cone. If you find that you have a negative unit margin (that is, you
lose money on every ice cream cone you sell), you must stop every-
thing and revisit your cost and revenue variables. Don't increase
volume until your margin is positive.

One you have a positive profit margin on each unit, you can increase your profit by increasing volume. The next few chapters detail ways to do this.

QUESTIONS ON CHAPTER 5: MAXIMIZING REVENUE

1. Explain the differences between revenue, reimbursement, cost, price, charge, and profit.

2. Define the following spreadsheet categories:
   - Gross Revenue

   - Total Net Revenue

   - Revenue per Unit

   - Revenue Percent

3. Explain what a payer category is. List some of the payer categories from your organization.

4. What is a payer mix and how does it affect revenue?

5. Differentiate between fixed-fee and fee-for-service reimbursement.

6. Differentiate between charge-based and cost-based reimbursement.

7. Describe ways to influence revenue

   •   Before the sale

   •   During the sale

   •   After the sale

8. Describe a pricing strategy in common use in your business.

9. What is unit profitability and how does it relate to volume?

6

Increasing Sales Volume

PRINCIPLES OF PROFITABILITY

Before we get into building sales volume, let's reiterate the basic underlying principle of profitability: First ensure a positive margin on every unit, then increase the number of units you sell.

I swore I wouldn't use that tired old joke in this book, but it seems inevitable. This particular version is my father's: Two guys went to El Centro and found cantaloupes in the field selling for $1.00 each. They loaded up their truck and brought them back to San Diego, where they sold them for $1.00 each. They were disappointed to find they hadn't made any money. "Well, you know what this means," said the first guy. "Next time we need a bigger truck."

When you're losing money on every sale, you'll never make it up in volume! Before you start to build volume, make sure you have a positive unit margin.

NOT-FOR-PROFIT SALES FUNCTIONS

So what do sales mean to a not-for-profit organization? This is one of the stickier concepts in this book. Many NFPs have products that don't seem to demand sales. What do sales have to do with a lifeguard, or an IRS agent, or the chairperson of this year's charity ball?

Let's look at one example. If you're a fire chief, do you really want to increase your sales? Don't jump to assume that this means you want to increase fires. What you really sell is fire suppression, or putting out the fire. You sell the ounce of prevention, plus a pound of cure just in case. So, you really do want to increase the demand for your service; you want people to buy your service in case they need it. You want to sell the value of having a fire department, even if you don't want to increase the number of times it is actually used.

Here are some more examples: Say you're a minister. How would you look at sales volume? Sales to you means increasing the size of your congregation. If you're a school principal, your sales volume would be enrollment. The department of motor vehicles has a wider variety of products, so its sales would be the number of users of each of its services. So, the not-for-profits still follow the for-profit model; it just takes a little more thought to figure out what it is you want to sell.

All that said, now let's look at ways to increase sales.

WAYS TO INCREASE SALES VOLUME

In the last several chapters you learned how to ensure a positive unit margin. Now we're ready to begin building sales volume. There are several ways to do this.

> To increase profit on a product, you have to increase its popularity.
>
> —*Andy Rooney*

Penetration

Penetration means penetrating beyond your slice of the pie to get a bigger market share. It is done by convincing existing customers to use more of your product, or getting "undecideds" to select you, or luring customers away from the competition.

Far and away the easiest and least expensive way to increase sales volume is to provide superlative customer service. I was recently asked by a hospital to increase the number of orthopedic admissions through its emergency department. The hospital had a stable group of high-quality orthopedic surgeons who used both its emergency department and other facilities in the community. When I talked to the customers (the orthopedists), they said, "The staff is never there when you need them."

This was a challenging problem. The staff members had no incentive to change. They were quick to tell me how busy they were trying to take care of the patients, and they had a hard time seeing one physician group as their "customer." I first had to convince them that the orthopedists were also trying to take care of their patients, and were in fact on the same team. Then I explained the role orthopedics played in the bigger picture of the hospital: it was the biggest revenue source and its profit paid for many of the hospital's charity functions. And the orthopedists had the highest-quality orthopedic service in town, with the number one market share for several years. In essence, the orthopedists were providing the profit that paid the staff members' salaries so that they could take care of patients.

To make a long story short, I convinced them that they wanted to provide exceptional service to this group, and asked them to do the following: Whenever an orthopedist enters the emergency department, just go up and say, "Hello, Dr. So-and-So," and offer to help. That's all. No special training or unusual work request. Just make eye contact and offer to help the doctor care for the patients. Well, it took a few weeks of reinforcing this, and encouraging, and persisting, but the outcome was worth it. The doctors noticed the change immediately, and after six months, the orthopedic admissions through the emergency department had increased by 17 percent.

You just can't say enough about customer service. Schools should consider ways to make it easier for working parents to arrange conferences, or talk with teachers and principals. Government offices can create directories so citizens know exactly how to locate the service they want. The best example of outstanding customer service is found at Nordstrom: its personnel manual is reportedly a single paragraph that says, in essence, just do whatever it takes to keep the customer satisfied. The Nordstrom model transformed the retail industry because it showed that outstanding customer service can draw customers from the competition despite elite prices. If you can develop in your NFP staff the mind-set that encourages them to bend over backwards to anticipate their customer needs and find innovative ways to meet them, even if it means doing something that's not in the standard policy, this will do more to increase your volume than any amount of glossy three-color brochures.

Product Development

Product development means changing the product so that existing customers use more of it. It can include finding new ways to package or sell existing products, or developing entirely new products of interest to existing customers.

What products are your competitors offering that you don't? Ask your customers what their needs are. What would they like to see? How can you meet those needs? Watch your customers. Look at their behaviors to identify service opportunities.

Market Development

Market development means attracting new buyers who aren't currently your customers. It is done by developing new products that will appeal to members of the new markets you want to enter.

Ask yourself the following questions: What special skills, facilities, and/or equipment do I have that enable me to perform my current services? What other things might these skills, facilities, and equipment be used for? For example, if I now run a public library that has a travel room with a lot of travel videos, might I develop that into a travel club for the local senior citizen group? What parallel markets exist for the services I now provide? For example, if I now sell meals for patients, might I also sell meals to their visitors? Remember, though, that new product ideas must enhance revenue!

MARKETING AND THE MARKETPLACE

By definition, marketing is "a total system of business activities that directs the flow of goods and services from producer to users, in order to satisfy customers and accomplish company goals." Marketing is *not* just another word for advertising. Marketing *is* a broad business activity that encompasses what business schools call the "4 Ps."

The 4 Ps of Marketing

Product: Creating or providing items or services that meet the customers' needs and wants

Place: Accessing, distributing, finding ways to get the product to the customer

Promotion: Packaging, advertising, and using other ways to call attention to the product

Price: Strategically setting an asking price, discounting, and leveraging to optimize revenue

The marketing process begins with market research and analysis and proceeds with strategy development, plan implementation, and finally evaluation of results and modification of strategy (see Figure 6–1).

Marketing is a system that provides transactions between the organization and its target audiences (see Figure 6–2). These transactions include communication to the customer, delivery of goods and services, payment of fees, and feedback information from the customer. The marketplace is the arena in which those goods and services are exchanged.

Marketing is done to persuade members of the marketplace to select more of the company's products or services. Marketing is the tool used to build volume.

Figure 6–1 The Marketing Process

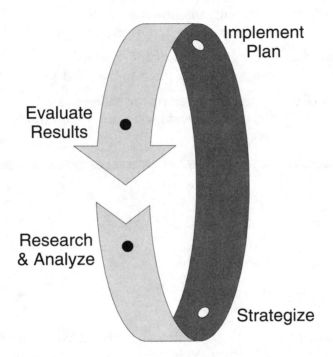

Figure 6–2 The Marketing System

MARKET RESEARCH

A very large component of any marketing function is research. It is essential to your success that you know your market, your customers, and your competition. There are a number of official, unofficial, and outright creative sources for gathering this kind of information.

Take the case of a young company just starting out in the business of selling disposable medical products to hospitals. Some of its eager managers made a practice of going through hospital trash bins to find out what nondisposable items were routinely discarded. Their premise was: If they're willing to throw away an expensive item rather than clean it, they're probably willing to pay for a disposable model if we can make one. That company is now a Fortune 500 company with a very healthy reputation in the industry.

WHO ARE YOUR CUSTOMERS?

Knowing who your customers are isn't always as easy as it sounds. Sometimes a company knows without doubt who its customers are. More often, it has to conduct an extensive analysis to find out. Do you know who your customers are? Go back to your mission statement. Why are you in business? Who buys what you sell? Who makes the actual buying decision? Is the buyer also the user? Is there an intermediary (such as a distributor) who influences the buying decision?

You undoubtedly have more than one customer group. For a hospital, the primary customers include the patients, the physicians, and the payers. There are many other customers, such as families/ friends and the hospital staff, but these are the three primary customers. The patient is the one who actually uses the service, but the physician is often the one who makes the buying decision, and the payer is the one who must ultimately be satisfied.

Figure 6–3 shows four revealing charts that were created from customer profile information. To compile customer profile information, list all your customer groups in order of volume and profit potential. For example, which of the ice cream customers bought

Figure 6–3 Customer Profile Information

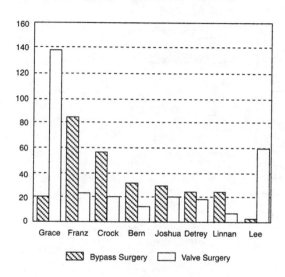

A) MD Volume by Product

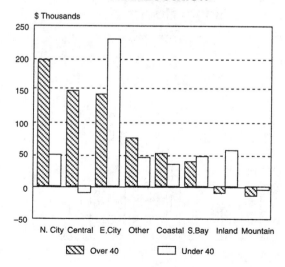

B) Gain/Loss by Age and Location

Figure 6–3 continued

C) Surgical Admissions Gain/Loss

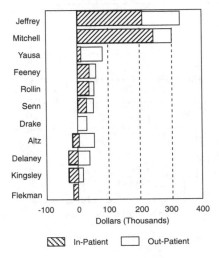

D) Preferred Operating Room Hours

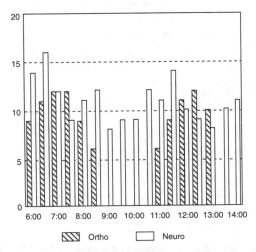

the most ice cream? Was it the seniors, the children after school, the families on the weekends, the gourmets in the late evening, or your cheap friends? For each group, you should prepare a customer group profile that tells you how often they buy, how profitable their purchases are, and the buying patterns they display. When you're done, you'll be able to describe your market in terms of size for each group and for the market as a whole.

WHO IS THE COMPETITION?

In much the same way you profile your customers, you should also know your competition, since that's a large part of the equation for volume. The market, which is the sum of all the people who might buy your service, is often described in terms of a pie, with slices going to each seller. You have your slice, or percentage of the market, and the other slices belong to your competition. The goal is to make your slice bigger by taking buyers away from the competition. If the market size is fixed, that is, the pie is of a set size, you must know your competition and its strengths and weaknesses in order to control your own profitability.

For example, if you run the local library and think of your business as book loans, you will want to know how many other libraries there are in your community, because they would be your direct competitors for business. But what if you think of your business as providing entertainment? Now your competition might also include bookstores, video rental companies, and any other business that your customers might turn to in lieu of your library. The better you understand your business, your customers, and your competition for those customers, the more effectively you will serve your market and the more profitable you will become.

So, who are your competitors? Who else sells what you sell? If you closed tomorrow, to whom would your customers turn for your service?

For each competitor you identify, create a competitor profile (Exhibit 6–1) that answers the following questions:

1. Which of my products does this competitor provide?

Exhibit 6–1 Competitor Profile

(Complete 1 Page for Each Competitor)

COMPETITOR _____   RANKING _____

1. Which of my products does this competitor provide?

2. How important are these products to

    My Business   My Competitor's Business

3. How do I compare with this competitor?

	My Business	My Competitor
Volume		
Price		
Service		
Quality		
Innovation		

4. What are my competitor's:

    Strengths   Weaknesses

5. What is my competitor's global strategy? How can I avert it?

2. How important are these products to my business? To my competitor's business?

3. How do I compare with this competitor in areas of volume, price, service, quality, and innovation?

4. What are my competitor's strengths? Weaknesses?

5. What is my competitor's global strategy? How can I avert it?

To create these profiles, you will want to research existing resources, as well as create new information sources such as internal information hotlines. Most NFPs keep an eye on their main competitor, but they do so informally. Let's say you run one of several NFPs that provide services for the homeless. You all do good work, but you compete for the limited funds available from government grants and philanthropy. If you find out that a large demonstration project is being contemplated for your city, you'll want to know which of your competitors is going to bid on it and what each has to offer. This information is important so that you can prepare an application of equal or greater attractiveness, thus to ensure your participation in this project.

You might informally ask your assistant, who used to work for your competitor, whether he or she knows what the competitor will be presenting in its application. Or one of your case workers might mention a conversation overheard at a community meeting that pointed out a weakness in your position. You want to take control of this informal process by giving your staff an organized way to share this information with you. For instance, you might set up an internal telephone hot line for ideas and information pertaining to the organization's competitive position. Or you could let all your staff members know in the staff meeting that they can send you market information directly on your electronic mail.

Industry has been using this strategy for years. It's called industrial espionage, and it's big business. There's talk now about converting some of our country's cold war espionage expertise into more commercial veins by engaging the Central Intelligence Agency in this type of application. What I'm talking about here isn't as tricky, but it's just as valuable.

Let's say your organization runs a series of summer programs for children. This field is becoming increasingly competitive as churches, youth groups, schools, and civic organizations vie with local entertainment groups for revenues from the summer crowd. You need to find out what the kids (and their parents) want so you can give it to them. But you also want to know what your competitors are doing so you can stay one step ahead of them.

First, you should call all the competitors you know and put your own children on their mailing lists (then quickly order a filing cabinet to store all the flyers you will get). Next, let all your employees know that you're starting an information hot line. Pick an internal phone line and give them that number. Tell them to call if they hear about any new and innovative ideas. Then keep track of all the leads. A single tidbit might not mean much, but as you compile data from all your sources you'll begin to see glimpses of your competitors' strategies. That's priceless.

Once you have an idea what's going on in your marketplace, you can construct a pie chart (Figure 6–4) that illustrates the total market share for your business, showing the appropriate slice for each of your competitors, and a slice for the untapped market share.

PRODUCT PORTFOLIO

All products have life cycles. They have an initial emerging stage during which their growth is slow, then they peak in sales, and eventually fade off into the sunset. All products do this. Their growth/decline curves may be different shapes, they may grow and age at different speeds, some may peak higher or faster than others, and some may fade so slowly that they seem to go on forever. But they all fade eventually.

For a business to remain healthy as products fade, it must continually seek new products to add to its portfolio. Depending on each particular product's inherent potential and its current position on the life cycle curve, it can be a winner or a loser.

The Boston Consulting Group (BCG) illustrated this concept in a now-famous grid, the "Growth Rate–Market Share Matrix" (see Figure 6–5). The BCG grid identifies four categories of products:

1. **Cash Cows:** These are high-potential, lucrative products that are at a peak in their growth cycle.

Figure 6–4 Market Share Analysis—Smoking Cessation Market

A) Compared to Last Year

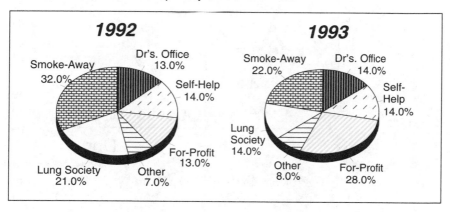

B) New vs Repeat Business

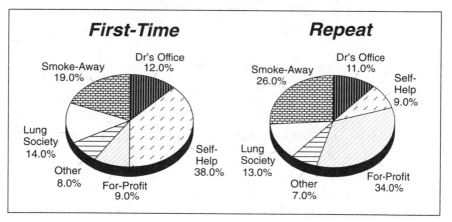

Figure 6–5 Product Portfolio Matrix (BCG Grid)

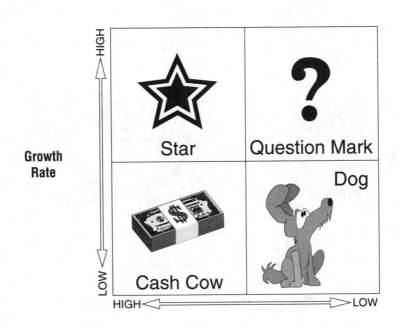

BCG Grid

---

2. **Dogs:** As the name implies, these products are eating up more than they bring to the table.
3. **Stars:** Rising stars are early in their life cycle but with great potential to become cash cows.
4. **Question Marks:** This category is for products that might do well, but equally might fail.

Product portfolio management involves adding, cultivating, and harvesting products based on the BCG grid, or a similar categorization. Should you hold on to a Question Mark? How long can the Cash Cow continue feeding the Dogs? Can you afford to keep the Dogs until the Star has risen a little higher? Which Question Mark will be your next Cash Cow? As with all gambling strategies, the trick is to "know when to hold 'em and know when to fold 'em." You can improve your odds of success by increasing the number of cards in your hand (products in your portfolio).

STRATEGIC MARKETING PLAN

Because each product has its own margin and its own buyer, your marketing approach will have to vary with each product. As you develop a marketing plan for each product, begin with a systematic analysis of the product's strengths and weaknesses. The most common format for this analysis is the **S-W-O-T** tool (Exhibit 6–2), which simply asks you to list *Strengths, Weaknesses, Opportunities,* and *Threats* for your product. Strengths and weaknesses are

---

Exhibit 6–2 S-W-O-T Analysis

STRENGTHS *Internal*	WEAKNESSES *Internal*
OPPORTUNITIES *External*	THREATS *External*

considered to be internal, while threats and opportunities are external. Some people call this the "WOT'S Up" model. Another, simpler
model is the **W-I-S-E** matrix (Exhibit 6–3).

All of these tools simply ask you to address methodically both
internal and external strengths and weaknesses for your NFP
organization and/or its product(s) for the purpose of identifying
potential strategic opportunities that will become the basis for a
comprehensive campaign to position and move your products
competitively in your marketplace.

Countless factors can influence your ability to respond to market
opportunities (see Figure 6–6). Each of these variables should be
considered while you develop your marketing strategy. Your conclusions following your analysis should address questions such as
the following:

1. Are there market segments or niches that are weakly held by
   competitors? How might you steal that market?

Exhibit 6–3 W-I-S-E Analysis

	STRENGTHS	WEAKNESSES
INTERNAL		
EXTERNAL		

Figure 6–6 Factors That Affect Marketing Effectiveness

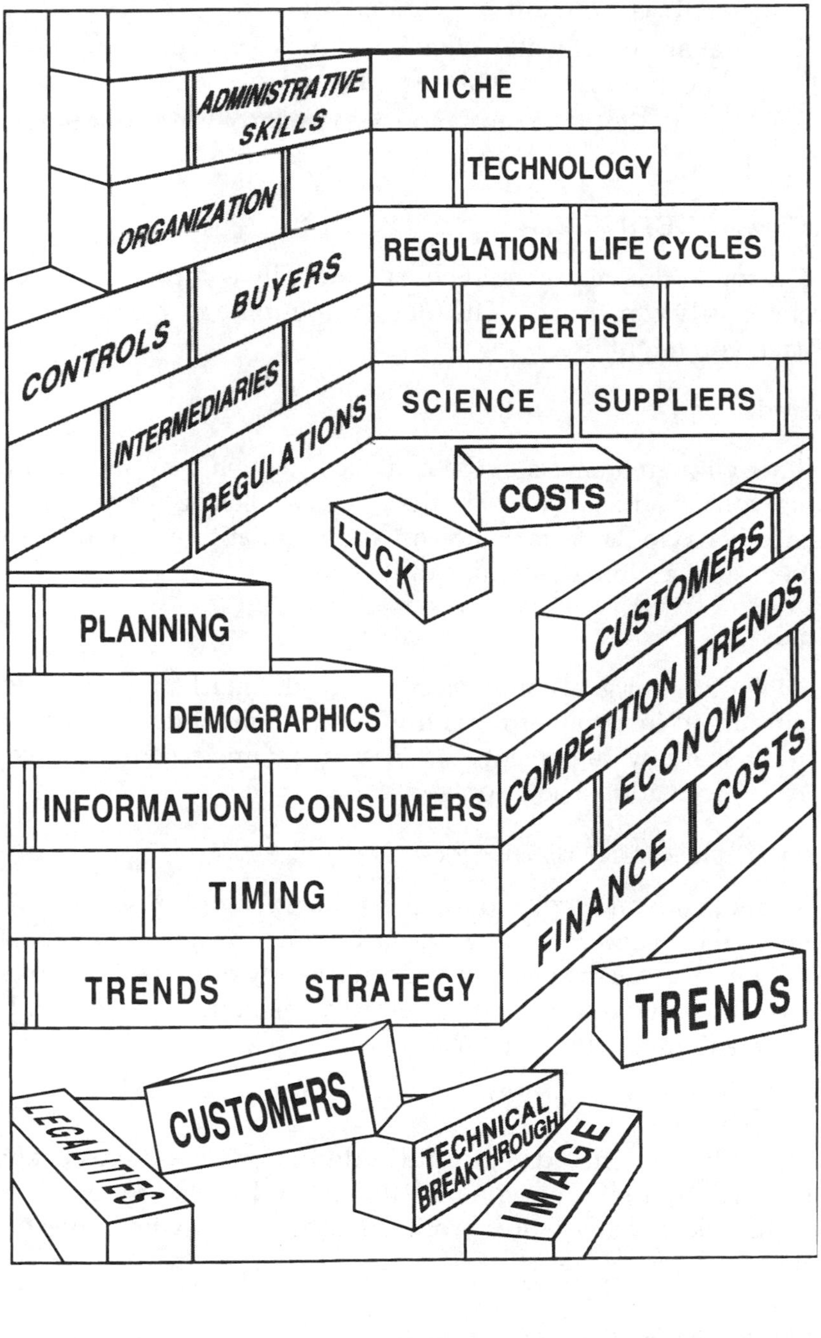

2. What portion of the market is unclaimed? Why has no one taken it? How might you commandeer it?

3. What are your goals? What objectives, strategies, and tactics will position you to achieve your goals?

Armed with those thoughts, you are ready to write your marketing plan.

THE MARKETING PLAN

The marketing plan should be methodically composed and comprehensively constructed. The following outline is one generic approach you might use.

Introduction

Start with an analysis of the context in which you hope to promote your products. What are the issues at play? Summarize consumer behavior, referral patterns, the competitive arena, related advertising, and market opportunities.

Goals

Spell out your goals and objectives for the marketing campaign. Define them in terms of measurable outcomes, such as "increase market share by 10 percent," or "increase name recognition by 25 percent," or "add 20 new contracts."

Evaluation

Think in advance how you will evaluate the response you get. If your goal is to add 20 new contracts, how will you know whether a new contract was the result of your marketing efforts or just coincidence? How will you know whether your name recognition has improved? Again, think in terms of outcomes.

Strategy

Your strategy should begin with a definition of your target audience. Whom are you hoping to attract, and what is their demographic and psychographic profile? The answers to these questions will determine the direction your tactics take.

Next, select specific strategies to attract prospects; identify those who are qualified (able to buy); and provide mechanisms for communication with them, first when the prospects respond to your message, and then how the business will respond back to the prospects. Create a way to engage the targets in dialogue and to manage future interactions.

Develop a strategy for the creative component of your campaign. What will be the tone, image, and identity of your message? Your image will be the first, and often most powerful, message to potential markets. As you design your image, ask yourself what key concepts you want to convey. For example, many NFPs would be damaged by "glitzy" materials that look as if the entire year's budget (paid for by taxes) went into a single brochure. Some NFPs (such as schools, mental health agencies) will want to convey a serious, competent image, while others (children's museum, youth groups) might want to sell fun. Decide the tone your customers will want, and develop an image that communicates that tone. Consider also ways to integrate components and maintain your message over time.

Finally, select an advertising strategy that optimizes mix of media, including selection of media type (TV, radio, outdoor, print, etc.) and specifics (stations, locations, time periods, etc.) most likely to reach your target audience. If your NFP provides literacy training, you might select a medium that does not require reading (radio, TV) so that your potential students will be able to receive your message. When I use the drive-through automated teller machine at my bank, I am puzzled by the fact that someone has gone to great trouble and expense to convert the control panel to Braille, without considering that a user who needs Braille is unlikely to use the drive-through ATM.

NFPs have one advantage over for-profits in the marketing arena, and that's in the use of public service announcements, or PSAs. If you develop a good relationship with the station manager, you can occasionally parlay a single PSA opportunity into professional help with a media plan. Experts can provide priceless guidance in selecting the proper form to reach your audience. For example, they may suggest that you need a targeted mailing, instead of mass-media advertising such as radio or TV.

Creative Content

Creative is the marketing term for the artistic component of your campaign. None of the artwork itself should be developed until your strategic plan has been formulated. The strategy should drive the creative content of your ads, brochures, and miscellaneous marketing supplements such as pins, stickers, and the like. The artwork should augment and complete the strategy; it should never be a substitute for it.

Time and again I have had ad agencies present me with attractive ads, which I promptly reject when they can't tell me who the target is, or what the strategic objective is. You don't have to know what the answers are, but you should know the questions to ask. If the agency can't give you an answer that makes you comfortable, find another agency.

Time Frames

You'll need a schedule that specifies the milestones throughout the run of the campaign. Allow sufficient time for planning, creative brain-storming, approvals, launch, and media run. Then add another 15 percent for evaluating whether or not you accomplished your goals.

Costs

Construct a budget that accounts for all planning, creative, and production costs such as printing or filming. Include cost of media space and/or air time, and any peripheral costs such as events or special activities. Then add administration costs to complete your cost profile for the campaign.

Most importantly, calculate a Return on Investment for your campaign. Go back to your original goals to see your unit of measure for outcomes. For example, let's say your goal was to bring in 20 new contracts. Now divide your total campaign costs by 20, for a per-contract advertising cost. If your costs came to $160,000 for the campaign, you should allocate a marketing cost of $8,000 to each contract. Then ask the final question, "Is it worth $8,000 to get a new contract?" If the answer is yes, you have justified your marketing costs.

*   *   *

By definition, marketing is the process by which you influence transactions with your customers. At some point in any discussion of marketing, you begin to bump up against ethics. At issue is the question of influencing the buyer. Does influencing mean informing, persuading, pressuring, or coercing? That's the slippery slope that makes a lot of NFP managers look at marketing as distasteful and unethical. But it doesn't have to be that way. If your competitors establish marketing practices that violate your ethics, you don't have to feel pressured to follow suit.

I offer the advice of someone who has owned his own business for 14 years and built it into a highly successful organization with a national reputation for quality and excellence, "You have to do what's right, no matter what the other guy does." He has never had to do formal advertising. His secret: he always gives the customers a little more than they pay for, and the word-of-mouth marketing has given him the competitive edge.

SALES PLAN

Marketing and sales are inseparable; the goal of each is to increase volume. Marketing is selling (or convincing prospects to buy), but marketing does not necessarily include direct sales. Many NFPs (if not most) don't have a direct sales function; that is, they don't have salespeople who go out talking to customers and trying to get them to buy.

Depending on your type of service, you may need to include direct sales in your marketing strategy. If so, you will need to add a comprehensive sales plan to your marketing strategy. Sales strategy is a very intricate subject and could fill a book of its own. If your NFP needs direct sales, you should do additional research on the makings of a full sales plan. Briefly stated, you will want to include at least the three items listed below:

1. List all sales volume ideas generated, in order of volume opportunity and potential for accomplishment.

2. Determine how you might enhance your distribution system. Is there a way to improve customer access to your services? Is there a barrier between you and your customer that might be removed?

3. Define your sales force and outline the training and materials they will need.

You will also need specific sales goals, separate from your marketing goals. Construct realistic, measurable volume goals for your service. For example: Sell 2,500 home-catered meals within the first year.

CONCLUSION

You now know a lot about each of the three variables affecting profit. You know what they are, how to influence them, and how they work together to determine the profitability of your business. The next step is to learn how to monitor them on a daily basis so you are always in touch with your profitability.

QUESTIONS ON CHAPTER 6: INCREASING SALES VOLUME

1. Before trying to increase sales volume, you must first do what with the unit margin?

2. What would constitute "sales" in your particular NFP business?

3. How might you improve customer service in your organization?

4. How might you ask your customers what they need, so that you can develop new products to increase your volume?

5. How might you expand your current products/services to reach additional customers (and produce additional revenue)?

6. Explain what marketing is and how it is more than just advertising.

7. Describe the following components of the marketing process:

- Market Research

- Marketing Strategy

- Plan Implementation

- Evaluation

8. Define the customers of your NFP. Who buys what you sell? Compile Customer Profile data (Figure 6–1) for each of your customer groups.

9. List all of your customer groups in order of volume potential.

10. Quantify market size for each customer group and for your total market.

11. Who are your competitors? If you closed tomorrow, where would your customers go? Complete a Competitor Profile (Exhibit 6–1) for each of your competitors.

12. Analyze the market share for your business and for each of your competitors (including untapped market share). Draw a pie chart of your market. Determine how big your slice is and who else has slices in your pie.

13. How could you make your slice bigger? How might you increase the size of your whole pie? How might you get slices of another pie?

14. List trends that you might expect to influence future market size. For example, consider trends in population, industry regulation, reimbursement, scientific knowledge, etc.

15. For the products in your organization, decide where each is in its own product life cycle. Which ones are new and rising? Which ones are just peaking? Which are fading, and when will they be gone? When should you begin planning for replacement products?

16. Complete a strategic analysis grid (S-W-O-T or W-I-S-E) for your organization as a whole and for each of your key products.

17. Begin to draft a marketing plan for one or more of your products:

    • What are your goals?

    • How will you evaluate achievement of goals?

    • Who is your target audience?

    • What is your message?

    • What strategies might you use to deliver your message?

    • What do you want the target to do in response to your message?

    • What creative component (media, etc.) might you employ?

    • What is your time frame?

    • How much should you budget?

18. Think of new uses for existing products/services: What special skills, facilities, and/or equipment do you have that might be used for additional services? What other markets exist for those services?

19. Think of new products/services: What products do your competitors offer that you don't? Do your customers have needs that aren't currently being met?

20. Can you penetrate new markets? Are there market segments or niches that are weakly held by competitors? How might you steal that market? What portion of the market is unclaimed? Why has no one taken it? How might you commandeer it?

21. How can you enhance existing markets? How might you influence customers to use more of your products/services? Are there other categories of people who might also benefit?

22. Do some of your services inadvertently limit your volume? For example, do you offer à la carte foods that preempt selection of the more profitable full-meal plan?

23. Will your organization need direct sales to increase volume? If so, begin developing your sales plan.

7

Monitoring Performance

GOALS OF FINANCIAL REPORTING

Now that you have all the pieces to the profit formula, you'll want to find ways to monitor your accomplishments in each of the variable areas. There are countless traditional mechanisms for this, and I'll suggest some others that aren't so traditional.

Standard financial reports don't vary much between profit companies and not-for-profit organizations. The basics are all the same, and they all relate back to the Profit Formula and its three variables: cost, revenue, and sales volume. As you begin to look at the various accounting reports, don't be intimidated by them. Just remember, you're not an accountant, you're a leader.

You don't have to be able to calculate a profit and loss statement; that's what accountants are for. Your job is to know how to read it, and then use the information it contains to make leadership decisions.

Let's start with the basics. What are the goals of financial reporting; why do you need financial reports? Here are three important purposes:

1. **To Measure Financial Performance:** In other words, are we making a profit? The key variables will be cost, revenue, and sales volume.
2. **To Monitor Changes in Financial Performance:** You're going to want to keep an eye on trends in your profitability. To do

that, you'll want to monitor each reporting period as compared to past performance.

3. **To Target Operational Changes:** You wouldn't be much of a manager if all you did was watch the profit go up and down. The real goal here is to manipulate the operational variables so you can begin to increase your profit. The financial reports help you target which operational areas are most amenable to profit enhancement.

To do these things, you'll want to monitor the following five areas:

1. **Spending:** You're familiar with spending. All managers want to know how much money they have to spend. Otherwise, they wouldn't know when they've spent or overspent it.

2. **Profit Performance—Now:** How profitable are we right now, today? What is our current status on cost, revenue, and sales volume?

3. **Profit Performance—Past:** How profitable were we yesterday, last month, last year? Again, the variables are cost, revenue, and sales volume.

4. **Profit Performance—Future:** How profitable are we likely to be tomorrow? This is particularly important when projecting the likely success of a new venture, or when trying to secure a bank loan.

5. **Cash Availability—Now and Short-Term:** Being profitable is different from having money. Try buying a newspaper with a $5,000 Certificate of Deposit. If a donor has pledged $1 million in unrestricted funds, it will make a big difference whether the funds come in at one time or in quarterly installments. Can you spend the entire $1 million, or is it given as an endowment, so that your access to the money will be at today's interest rate? How are your expenses distributed? Is the bond due in 12 equal monthly payments or in one payment yearly? Are you lucky enough (or smart enough) to correlate your quarterly gifts with your quarterly bond payment? It's critical to balance the cash-in and cash-out flow so you can meet weekly payroll and pay the bills.

Figure 7–1 Financial Reports

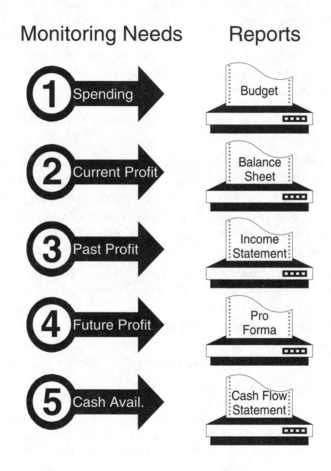

That's essentially it, just the five major reporting needs described above. Coincidentally, there is a standard financial report to monitor each of those key areas.

Exhibit 7–1 Sample Budget

	North Shores Community Center		
Department	Budgeted Costs	Actual Costs	Variance
General Administration	$60,000	$62,534	($2,534)
Fund Raising	75,000	77,598	(2,598)
Program Activities	350,000	347,991	2,009
Public Relations	150,000	123,997	26,003
TOTAL	$635,000	$612,120	$22,880

Budget

The budget tells you how much money you have to spend, provides an accounting of how much you have actually spent, and then gives you the difference, called a variance. Most people are familiar with departmental budgets, which itemize all revenues and expenses in detail. Every cost is given its own line on the budget, thus the term "line-item expense" (Exhibit 7–1).

Balance Sheet

The Balance Sheet (Exhibit 7–2) is like a snapshot of your company's current profit profile. It is a slice in time that tells you how much debt you have against how many assets you have at one discrete point in time. Notice that they're no longer called costs and revenues. Instead they're called assets and liabilities. Don't get nervous . . . they're still resources you have and debts you owe.

Exhibit 7–2 Sample Balance Sheet

CENTER FOR CHILDHOOD DISEASES

Midwest Children's Hospital

Consolidated Balance Sheet
September 30, 1994

ASSETS

Current Assets

Cash	127,901
Accounts Receivable	169,695
Current Portion of Bond Payment Fund	302,419
Other Current Assets	15,120
Total Current Assets	615,135

Property and Equipment

Building and Land Improvements	6,009,982
Equipment	2,594,189
Total Property & Equip	8,604,171
Less Depreciation and Amortization	(2,502,795)
Net Property & Equipment	6,101,376

Deferred Bond Insurance Costs, Net   208,740

$6,925,251

LIABILITIES AND FUND BALANCES

Current Liabilities

Accounts Payable	187,790
Accrued Payroll and Employee Benefits	108,398
Accrued Interest	156,820
Deferred Revenue and Grant Advances	295,457
Current Portion of Long-Term Debt	165,000
Total Current Liabilities	913,465

Long-Term Debt   4,353,000

Total Liabilities   5,266,465

Fund Balances

Unrestricted	408,786
Restricted	1,250,000
Total Fund Balances	1,658,786

$6,925,251

You might expect that the Balance Sheet would balance between the assets and the liabilities. However, NFPs rarely produce exactly as much revenue as costs (nobody is that good at managing money). So, even though they don't set out to make a profit, they do in fact generate either a positive or negative balance for the reporting period.

For-Profit companies account for this excess (or loss) in a section called "Stockholder Equity." For-profits are designed to produce a profit, and stock is the format they use for distributing it. Since stock has a financial value, it must be included in the Balance Sheet in the same way other assets are. Stockholder Equity also includes the amount of money the firm has received in exchange for its stock, as well as the "retained earnings," or profits earned by the firm over its lifetime that have not yet been distributed to its owners in the form of dividends.

By contrast, NFPs don't have stock or stockholder equity, and they aren't legally able to distribute excess earnings to individuals. They use a "Fund Balance" section on the Balance Sheet to account for excess revenues (or loss). The Fund Balance reflects the status of accumulated funds at the time indicated on the Balance Sheet. The result is that the NFP Balance Sheet always shows an equal balance between the Assets and the combined Liabilities/Fund Balance.

NFPs frequently receive contributions with the caveat that they be used only for a specific purpose, and management is required to restrict use of those funds to the purpose for which they were contributed. This accounting method, called "Fund Accounting," often causes the NFP Balance Sheet to have separate accountability for each of its funds. In all cases, liabilities are weighed against assets with excess (or deficit) balances shown in the Fund Balance.

Income Statement

The Income Statement (Exhibit 7–3) tells you how your company performed for a past period of time, such as your last fiscal year, or the last three months. It is similar to the Balance Sheet, but where the Balance Sheet is a snapshot in time, the Income Statement covers profit and loss performance for a given reporting period.

Exhibit 7–3 Sample Income Statement

St. Andrew's Shelter for the Homeless

ANNUAL INCOME STATEMENTS
For Fiscal Years 1993 and 1992

	FY93	FY92
REVENUES		
Federal Grants	4,934,015	5,020,227
Inter-Agency Transfers	1,731,518	1,674,463
Investment Income	64,775	16,585
Private Donations	154,303	209,096
Total Revenues	**6,884,611**	**6,920,371**
EXPENDITURES		
Wages and Benefits	3,968,211	4,090,764
Supplies and Services	1,889,721	1,849,978
Depreciation/Amortization	546,699	518,630
Interest	472,713	485,780
Total Expenditures	**6,877,344**	**6,945,152**
Excess of Revenue over Expenses	7,267	(24,781)
Fund Balances, Beginning of Year	2,057,975	2,082,756
Fund Balances, End of Year	2,065,242	2,057,975

Pro Forma

Like the Balance Sheet and the Income Statement, the Pro Forma (Exhibit 7–4) shows you debts and assets, and the difference between them. But the Pro Forma is a projection of what future profits might be, based on projected costs and revenues. The Pro Forma is one of management's most valuable tools for analyzing potential costs and benefits of new programs.

Cash Flow

The Cash Flow Statement (Exhibit 7–5) projects your use of cash and your sources of cash on a frequent (weekly or monthly) basis so that you can see how much liquid money you'll need, compared to how much you will have available, both now and in the short-term.

Exhibit 7-4 Sample Pro Forma

PROJECTED EXPENSES	Regional Educational Activities Drive (R.E.A.D.) Ballot Initiative Campaign						
	May	Jun	Jul	Aug	Sep	Oct	Total by Election Day
PERSONNEL							
Campaign Manager	1,000	1,000	1,000	1,000	1,000	1,000	6,000
Publicist	2,500	2,500	2,500	2,500	2,500	2,500	15,000
Precinct Workers	0	0	0	0	0	0	0
Office Staff	1,500	1,500	1,500	1,500	1,500	1,500	9,000
OPERATING EXPENSES							
Office Lease	1,000	1,000	1,000	1,000	1,000	1,000	6,000
Phones	200	200	200	200	200	200	1,200
Furniture Rental	75	75	75	75	75	75	450
Stationery, Business Cards	100	0	0	0	0	0	100
Office Supplies	200	50	50	50	50	50	450
Postage	20	150	150	150	150	150	770
Office Equipment	50	50	50	50	50	50	300
PUBLICITY							
Marketing Materials	50,000	0	0	0	0	0	50,000
Media (Air Time)	0	0	0	0	0	0	0
Media (Production)	20,000	0	0	0	0	0	20,000
MISCELLANEOUS							
Political Consultant	500	0	0	0	0	0	500
Legal Fees	500	0	0	0	0	0	500
Accounting Services	0	100	100	100	100	100	500
Entertainment	100	100	100	100	100	100	600
Travel Expenses	100	100	100	100	100	100	600
TOTAL EXPENSES	77,845	6,825	6,825	6,825	6,825	6,825	111,970

Exhibit 7–4 continued

PROJECTED REVENUES	May	Jun	Jul	Aug	Sep	Oct	Total by Election Day
Private Donations	4,000	5,000	6,000	7,000	7,000	6,000	35,000
Corporate Donations	2,000	5,000	5,000	5,000	2,000	2,000	21,000
Federal Matching Funds	6,000	10,000	11,000	12,000	9,000	8,000	56,000
TOTAL REVENUES	12,000	20,000	22,000	24,000	18,000	16,000	112,000
MONTHLY VARIANCE	(65,845)	13,175	15,175	17,175	11,175	9,175	30

Exhibit 7-5 Sample Cash Flow Statement

CLINICAL RESEARCH CENTER FOR AUTOIMMUNE DISEASES
Cash Management FY 94

	JAN	FEB	MAR	APR	MAY	JUN	JUL	AUG	SEP	OCT	NOV	DEC	Total
ACTIVITIES PROVIDING CASH													
Grants	325,132	265,190	315,190	325,132	265,190	205,248	325,132	265,190	205,248	325,132	265,190	205,248	3,292,222
Clinical Trials	1,950	39,488	1,950	39,488	1,950	39,488	1,950	39,488	29,289	1,950	15,619	1,950	214,560
Interest	27,016	27,016	27,016	27,016	27,016	27,016	27,016	27,016	27,016	27,016	27,016	27,016	324,192
Donations	27,132	27,132	27,132	277,132	27,132	27,132	27,132	27,132	27,132	27,132	27,132	27,132	575,584
Patient Fees	12,651	12,998	19,772	11,989	13,307	9,087	12,634	10,076	21,332	13,355	12,809	12,665	162,675
TOTAL	393,881	371,824	391,060	680,757	334,595	307,971	393,864	368,902	310,017	394,585	347,766	274,011	4,569,233
ACTIVITIES USING CASH													
Salaries & Benefits	160,759	158,141	158,141	147,086	147,086	143,475	148,890	148,890	148,887	140,242	140,242	132,766	1,774,605
Clinic Operations	70,208	84,189	71,800	68,901	71,323	84,122	79,890	80,045	86,444	83,887	91,231	89,665	961,705
Clinical Trials	39,501	39,501	39,501	51,128	51,128	51,128	51,128	51,128	50,368	50,368	47,112	56,112	578,103
Vivarium	1,380	1,380	1,380	4,038	4,038	4,038	4,038	4,038	4,038	4,038	4,038	4,038	40,482
Safety	7,375	7,375	7,375	7,375	7,375	7,375	7,375	7,375	7,375	7,375	7,375	7,375	88,500
Building Costs	38,300	38,300	38,300	38,300	38,300	38,300	38,300	38,300	38,300	38,300	38,300	38,300	459,600
Bond Payment	53,105	53,105	53,105	53,105	53,105	53,105	53,105	53,105	53,105	53,105	53,105	53,105	637,260
Capital Equipment	8,000	8,000	8,000	8,000	8,000	8,000	8,000	8,000	8,000	8,000	8,000	8,000	96,000
TOTAL	378,628	389,991	377,602	377,933	380,355	389,543	390,726	390,881	396,517	385,315	389,403	389,361	4,636,255
NET	15,253	(18,167)	13,458	302,824	(45,760)	(81,572)	3,138	(21,979)	(86,500)	9,270	(41,637)	(115,350)	(67,022)

It shows you the blips on your horizon so you can adjust your activities and possibly prepare yourself, like with a short-term bank loan to cover a high-cost period before big revenues come in.

The only way for you to get comfortable with financial reports is to start looking at them, analyzing them, adding up the various columns, and otherwise dissecting them until you know what's inside each one. Compare them to each other so that you can see how they are alike and how they are different. When you start, you'll find they all seem alike: they're all intimidating volumes of figures that make no sense. But as you pick through them you'll find they're really not difficult at all. The more you look at them, the more comfortable you'll become.

ACCOMPANYING NOTES

No matter what type of financial report you look at, it's likely to have tiny print at the bottom called "Notes to the Financials," or "Accompanying Notes," or some such phrase.

This is extremely important information, because it tells you what assumptions the accountants made when they constructed

Read the
SMALL PRINT!

(See Accompanying Notes)

that particular report. For example, it might tell you that it's a year's worth of data, but it was based on the first nine months, and then projected out for the full year. That's important. Or it might reveal a premise that's pretty ambitious, for instance, "this report assumes 100 percent market penetration." The notes give you the context in which the report should be interpreted. It is essential that you read the notes before drawing any conclusions from the report itself.

TREND REPORTING

It always amazes me when heavy-duty financial types can look at a financial report and comment, without taking into account the context in which the report was generated. Take, for example, the case of Katie Smith (see Figure 7–2). At noon Katie's temperature was 100.2 degrees. Is that good or bad? Well, that depends. What has her temperature been running? If it's been very high, a reading of 100.2 signals a break in the fever. But if it's been normal and suddenly spikes, that's another story.

Figure 7–2 Katie's Temperature is 100.2°

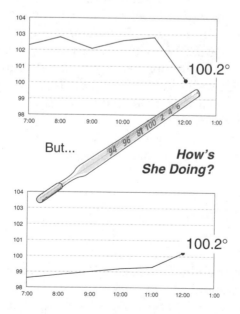

The same is true for financial reports. Without a series of reports to show you the trend, you really can't jump to conclusions on any single indicator. A wise manager will think ahead and implement standard reporting structures that will show performance patterns of key indicators in each of the three profit variables—cost, revenue, and volume—and then, to cap it off, a final trend report that will show overall profitability.

The first step in constructing such a trend report is to identify key variables for each of the categories. The variables will differ from one industry to the next, but every industry will have parameters in each of the three profit variables.

For each variable, construct a line graph showing performance on a regular basis, such as monthly. You can then select reports that will give you the specific information you seek and can examine them on a monthly basis, entering that month's data point into your line graph.

For example, let's say you want to monitor cost per unit of service. You set up a line graph showing cost on the vertical axis, and the months on the horizontal axis. Each month when you get a cost report, you enter that month's average cost per unit of service into the graph. And don't forget to notice the trend!

Select four to six variables each for cost, revenue, volume, and overall profitability (see Figure 7–3). You can cluster them so you have all the cost variables on the same page, revenue on another page, etc. If you're really obsessive you can design the graphs so that they all point in the same direction. That is, construct all the cost graphs so that a desirable trend has the line sloping down. Then when you glance at the cost page, all you have to do is notice that they all go down. Any that go up warrant a closer look. Of course, you'll want the revenue, volume, and profit graphs to show upward trends.

TREND VARIABLES

Cost

There are any number of financial parameters that reflect cost, and by now you should have a good sense of what cost figures are important in your NFP. Labor cost is essential in all industries, and

Figure 7–3 Hospital Sample Trend Report

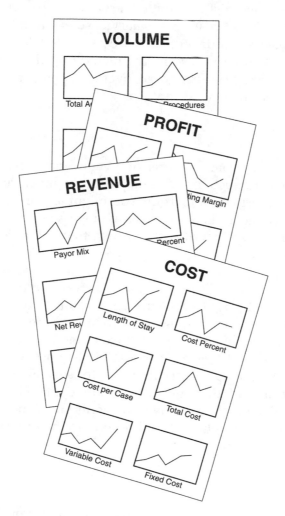

overhead (building, utilities, etc.) is also pretty standard. Then you will also have costs specific to your business. For example, a museum will have the cost of acquiring new pieces; and a day-care center might have costs of health, safety, and sanitation. Whatever your costs are, as you identified them in Chapter 4, you will now want to select key numbers by which to track trends.

Most of the generic financial indicators were covered in Chapter 4: total cost, average cost per unit of service, cost percent, total direct cost, total indirect cost, total salary cost, etc. In addition, you will want to select key indicators that are particularly meaningful to your business. Some of these might include productivity ratios, length of stay, average hourly wage, overhead percent, raw supply cost, turnover, occupancy percent, etc.

Revenue

The standard financial measures of revenue include net revenue, revenue percent, deductions percent, payer mix index, accounts receivable, and contribution margin. You might also monitor industry-specific revenue measures such as average revenue per sale, total amount of charitable write-offs, or cash-to-credit ratio.

Sales Volume

There are lots of ways to measure your volume. You might start with standard financial data such as total gross revenue or total units sold, but you will quickly advance to more specific information to differentiate between business maintenance and new business growth. For example, you could look to see how many consulting hours you sold this month, or you could slice the data differently and look at how many new clients you signed. The more you can design your volume trend to look to the future, the more secure your future will be.

Overall Profitability

For overall profitability you will want to monitor profit (operating) margin, both in actual cash amounts and as a percentage of net revenue. You may also choose to add graphs to your trend report showing overall profitability broken down by product lines, if you don't routinely examine these data in another format.

The trend report is a priceless management tool when properly constructed and maintained. The time you spend in setting it up will be worth the headaches in the end.

QUESTIONS ON CHAPTER 7: MONITORING PERFORMANCE

1. Explain each of the three basic goals (purposes) of financial reporting:
   - To Measure Financial Performance

   - To Monitor Changes in Financial Performance

   - To Target Operational Change

2. In order to accomplish the goals in question 1, you need to monitor at least five things. Explain each of these and why it's important:
   - Spending

   - Current Profit Performance

   - Past Profit Performance

   - Future Profit Performance

- Cash Availability

3. Describe each of the following financial reports. Tell what it does and what it doesn't do for your financial monitoring:

   - Budget

   - Balance Sheet

   - Income Statement

   - Pro Forma

   - Cash Flow Statement

4. Explain "Notes to Financials" or "Accompanying Notes." Tell what they do and why they're important.

5. Explain Trend Reporting, how it's done, and why.

6. For your NFP, outline what you would monitor on your Trend Report. Select key variables to monitor in each of the following areas:

- Cost

- Revenue

- Volume

- Overall Profitability

—— ❧ ——

8

Return on Investment

One of the biggest differences between for-profits and not-for-profits is the way they look at expenditures. In many not-for-profits, the month of May (for a July fiscal year) looms as the date by which they must spend whatever is left in their budget or they lose it. Departments scramble to find something to buy for $10,000, or whatever amount is left over. They know that their budget for next year will depend on how completely they spend this year's budget. The assumption is that if they didn't spend it, that must mean that they received too much last year, and thus will need (and be given) less next year. Hence, the end-of-year spending frenzy.

Almost never do managers examine the relative need for the purchase, or the cost, or the value. They aren't familiar with the concept of return on investment (ROI), and rarely examine the expenditure from that perspective. This is the ultimate question a manager must answer in each and every business situation: "What will be the return on my investment?"

CONCEPT OF ROI

In for-profit companies, all expenditures are related back to the ROI. For instance, instead of saying, "What shall we buy for this leftover $10,000," the for-profit would say, we'd like to buy new computer software that would eliminate the need for a clerk to process reports. The software costs $10,000. The clerk's salary is $13,000 per year, so the benefits (return) on the software package will outweigh the cost (investment).

The ROI concept says that expenditures are valued if they will result in more return than the original investment. That is, expenditures are made for the purpose of turning a profit. The greater issue to a for-profit is the availability of funds; i.e., do we have enough cash to take advantage of the opportunity?

CALCULATING ROI

To determine the ROI for an expenditure, you must first calculate all the costs, and then all the benefits (see Figure 8–1).

ROI is often expressed as a percentage. For example, if the benefits are equal to half again the cost, you would say you have an ROI of 150 percent; your benefits are 150 percent of your cost.

More often than not, your calculations will include both quantifiable elements (dollars) and intangibles such as strategic positioning, public image, etc. To the extent possible, you should try to translate the intangibles into dollars. For example, if a benefit is public image, try to determine what it would cost you to buy that public image. Then add that dollar amount into the equation in place of the less tangible description.

Figure 8–1 Calculating the Return on Investment

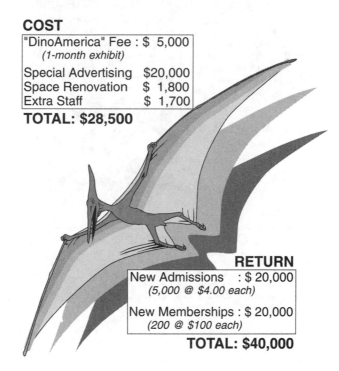

Carter Children's Museum
Dinosaur Animation Exhibit

COST

| "DinoAmerica" Fee : $ 5,000 |
| *(1-month exhibit)* |
| Special Advertising $20,000 |
| Space Renovation $ 1,800 |
| Extra Staff $ 1,700 |

TOTAL: $28,500

RETURN

| New Admissions   : $ 20,000 |
| *(5,000 @ $4.00 each)* |
| New Memberships : $ 20,000 |
| *(200 @ $100 each)* |

TOTAL: $40,000

Return on Investment: $11,500 (140%)

Figure 8–2 Claculating the Break-Even Anlaysis

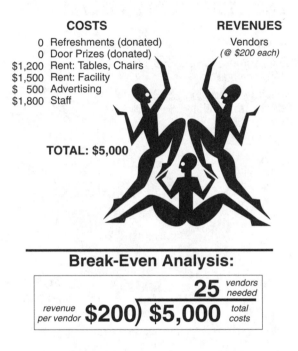

South Central
Health Fair

COSTS		REVENUES
0	Refreshments (donated)	Vendors
0	Door Prizes (donated)	*(@ $200 each)*
$1,200	Rent: Tables, Chairs	
$1,500	Rent: Facility	
$ 500	Advertising	
$1,800	Staff	

TOTAL: $5,000

Break-Even Analysis:

revenue per vendor $200) $5,000 *total costs*   →   **25** *vendors needed*

Break-Even Analysis

A very common calculation used to examine ROI is called a Break-Even Analysis (see Figure 8–2). This is the point at which all expenses are covered by benefit. Let's say you are running a conference and want to know how many attendees must register for you to break even on your costs. First you determine all your costs, then divide that number by the amount of a single registration. If your total costs are $2,000 and you are charging $35 per person, you divide $2,000 by $35 to find that you must have 57.14 registrants to cover your costs. The 58th person will begin to contribute to a profit for your conference.

Determining Pay-Back

Another way to look at ROI is to see how long it will take you to begin getting a pay-back on your investment. Let's say you want a piece of equipment that costs $20,000 more than your existing equipment. You project that you'll use it about ten times a month, and it will reduce your per-use cost by $50. That means you'll be

Bells 'n Whistles

Telephone System

COST

Price	$15,000
Warranty	$ 2,500
Installation	$ 2,500

TOTAL: $20,000

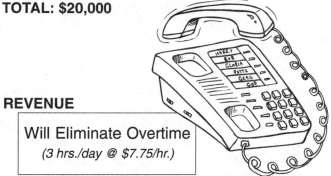

REVENUE

Will Eliminate Overtime
(3 hrs./day @ $7.75/hr.)

TOTAL: $500 per Month

Pay-Back Analysis:

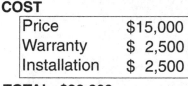

$$\frac{40 \text{ months}}{\$500 \overline{)\$20,000}}$$

monthly savings · *total cost*

This item will pay for itself in 40 months, or 3.3 years.
(Unfortunately, it's only guaranteed for 6-12 months.)

saving $500 per month with the new machine. At that rate, you'll pay back your initial investment in 40 months, or 3.3 years. Now consider the life expectancy of the machine. If it's designed to last 10 years, a 3.3-year pay-back would be great; it would give you another 6.7 years of benefit at $500 per month. But what if this particular machine will be outdated in 2 years? That changes the picture dramatically.

PROFITABILITY

So what does all this mean to you in a not-for-profit environment? As push comes to shove, the not-for-profits are increasingly expected to demonstrate return on investment. Those groups that provide the funds by which not-for-profits operate are demanding more accountability on the use of those funds, and are in fact expecting some return on their investment.

When the taxpayers (or your board members) say, "We're fed up and we just won't take it any more!" what they're really saying is, "We're no longer willing to pour our money down the drain . . . we want to see what it's buying." That's return on investment. It's accountability. It's an expectation that you get your money's worth. And it's inescapable. The days of free spending are over.

The winners in the new world will be those who can take the lessons from the for-profits and apply them to the not-for-profit environment. It's a mind-set, a different way of seeing things—not worse, just different. The challenge is to keep the qualities that make the not-for-profit world unique and valued, and add the accountability that goes with fiscal profitability. That is a powerful combination that can strengthen your organization and position it for success in a competitive economy.

Questions on Chapter 8: Return on Investment

1. Explain the concept of Return on Investment.

2. How is ROI used In for-profit companies?

3. How would you calculate ROI in your not-for-profit organization?

4. What is a Break-Even Analysis and how is it calculated?

5. How would you use a Break-Even Analysis in your not-for-profit organization?

6. What is Pay-Back?

7. When might you use the Pay-Back concept in your not-for-profit organization?

8. How would you calculate Pay-Back?

Index

(Boldface page numbers refer to figures.)

A

Accountability, profit, 19
Advertising, 87

B

Balance sheet, 101-103, **102**
  fund balance, 103
Billing procedures
  collections, 63
  in revenue enhancement, 62-63
Boston Consulting Group, 80-82
Break-even analysis, 120, **120**
Budget, 101, **101**
Business manager. *See also*
  Managers
  in creating mission statement, 5
  organizational assessment by, 5-7
  profit analysis by, 28-31

C

Capability, mission statement vs., 5
Capital
  assignable vs. unassignable, 43
  costs related to, 38, 43
Cash flow management, 99
  report for, 104, **107**, 108
Collections, 63
Community assessment, 12
Competition
  evaluation of, 77-80, **78**
  pricing and, 60
Contracting for services, 60-61
Contribution margin, **30**
Contributions, cash flow management of, 99
Corporate identity, 7-8
  in marketing strategy, 87
Cost
  accounting for, 45-48, **47**
  analyzing, 37-38

capital, 38
definition, 53
direct, **21**, 38, 40
fixed, **30**, 38-39
indirect, **21**, 38, 40-41
in marketing budget, 88-89
overhead, 38, 42-43, 49
payer mix analysis, **58**
per unit, 20, **21**, 46
in pro forma report, 104
in profit formula, 20-23
prospective analysis, 46-47, 48
retrospective analysis, 47-48
salary vs. nonsalary, **38**, 39
self-help questions, 50-51
as source of profit loss, 24-27
strategies for reducing, 48-49
total, **30**, 46
trend reporting, 110-112
unit, 110
variable, **30**, 38-39
Cost detail, **44**, 44-45, **45**
Cost percent, **30**, 46
Customer service, 68-70
Customers
  identifying, 1, 74-77
  market development, 70
  in mission statement perspective, 5
  profiling, **75-76**

D

Data collection and analysis. *See also* Financial reporting
in calculating costs, 46-48, **47**
in not-for-profit organizations, 28

product line profitability, 15, 16, 17
in profit analysis, 28
as revenue enhancement strategy, 61-62
in trend reporting, 109-112
Department manager, x, xi
Depreciation, 43

E

Equipment costs, 49
Ethical issues, 89
Excess reserves, vii

F

Fee-for-service systems, 56
Financial reporting
  accompanying notes, 108-109
  areas to monitor for, 99-101
  reports generated in, **100**, 101-108
  role of, 97-99
  self-test questions, 113-115
  trend analysis, 109-112
Fixed cost, **30**, 38-39
Food services, 16
For-profit organizations, vii-viii
  balance sheet reporting in, 103
Fund accounting, 103

G

Goal-setting
  in marketing plan, 86

mission statement for, 3-5, 11
in sales plan, 90
Government services, 69
Grant applications, 48
Green, Celia, 27
Gross revenue, **30**
Growth Rate-Market Share matrix, 80-83, **82**

H

Hospital
customer profile, 74, **76**
customer service, 68-69
food services, 16
indirect costs in, 41
profit analysis, 24-27
revenue concept in, 55-56

I

Income statement, 103, **104**
Insurance, 43
Interest, 43

L

Labor cost, 110-111
Leases, 49
Libraries, 77
Loans, interest cost in, 43

M

Mail services, **45**
Maintenance costs, 49
Managers. *See also* Business managers

business skills needed by, 1-3
organizational assessment by, x, xi
Margin, **30**
Marketing. *See also* Sales
4 Ps, **71**
advertising in, 87
competitor profile, 77-80, **78**
corporate identity in, 87
costs, 88-89
creating corporate identity for, 7-8
customer identification, 74-77
definition, 70
direct sales in, 89-90
ethical issues in, 89
Growth Rate-Market Share matrix, 80-83, **82**
identifying market share, 80, **81**
market development, 70
market penetration, 68-70
mission statement in, 5
in not-for-profit environment, 1
plan outline, 86-89
process, 71, **72**
public service announcements in, 87
research, 74
role of, 71
S-W-O-T analysis, **83**, 83-84
sales and, 89
self-help questions, 91-95
strategic planning, 83-86
W-I-S-E analysis, 84, **84**

Membership organizations, 61
Mission statement, 3-5, 11
Museums, 3-4

N

Not-for-profit organizations
  data collection practices in,
    28
  definition, vii
  efficient operation of, viii
  end-of-fiscal year spending,
    117
  funding trends, viii
  marketing in, 1
  membership fees, 61
  organizational structure, ix-x
  return on investment in, 122
  revenue in, 54, 103
  role of profit in, viii-ix, 8-10,
    19
  sales function in, 67-68

O

Operating gain/loss, vii, **30**
Organizational structure
  in cost-reduction strategies,
    48
  identifying product lines in,
    14-15
  overhead departments in, 42
  profit accountability in, 19-
    20
  for profitable operations, ix-
    x
  self-assessment, 12

Overhead, 38, 42-43
  costs, 49

P

Parks and recreation, ix, 5
Pricing, 56-60
  competition and, 60
  cost-plus method, 59
Pro forma report, 104, **105-106**
Product life-cycle, 80
Product line
  hospital, 24
  identification of, 14-15, 17
  organizational assessment,
    17-18
  product development, 70
  profit analysis, 13-14, 15-16,
    28-30, **33**
  profit per unit, 63
  services as, 14
  strategic marketing plan, 83-
    84
  unprofitable, 14
Product portfolio, 80-83
Productivity, 48
Profit
  assessment formula, 20-23
  cost-reduction strategies, 48-
    49
  data collection, 28
  definition, 20
  manipulating, **34**
  measuring, **34**
  monitoring of, 97-99
  in not-for-profit organiza-
    tions, vii, viii-x, 8-10, 19
  as obligation, 10

organizational analysis, 24-27

organizational sources, ix, 10

payer mix analysis, **57**

per unit, 63

principles of, 67

product line assessment for, 13-14, 15-16, 28-31, **33**

return on investment and, 122

self-help questions, 35-36

spreadsheet analysis, 27-28, **29**

trend reporting, 112

unit margin, 22, **22**

Profitability worksheet, 31, **32**

Public service announcements, 87

R

Reimbursement systems
charge-based, 56
cost-based, 56
fee-for-service, 56
fixed fee, 56
in identifying product lines, 14-15
payer mix analysis, 55, 56, **57-59**, 60
revenue types, 55-56

Return on investment
break-even analysis, 120, **120**
calculating, 118, **119**
concept of, 117-118
determining pay-back, 121-122
in marketing plan analysis, 88

in not-for-profit environment, 122

self-help questions, 123-124

Revenue
billing practices and, 62-63
contracting to increase, 60-61
data collection, 61-62
definition, 53
direct costs in production of, 40
enhancement strategies, 56-63
gross, **30**, 54
in not-for-profit environment, 54, 103
payer mix analysis, 60
per unit, 22, **22**, 54
percent, **30**, 54
pricing analysis, 56-60
in profit formula, 20-23
self-test questions, 64-65
total net, 54
trend reporting, 112
types of, 55-56

S

Salary costs, 39

Sales. *See also* Marketing
marketing and, 89
in not-for-profit environment, 67-68
plan for, 89-90
product development, 70
strategies to increase, 68-70

School system, 3, 5, 40, 69

Services vs. products, x, 14

Social services, competition in,
    79-80
Spreadsheet
    profit analysis, 27-28, **29**
    revenue analysis, 54
    terminology, **30**
Staffing, 48
Stockholder equity, 103
Substance abuse programs, 60
Supplies, 48
Surplus, vii

T

Total cost, **30**, 46

V

Variable cost, **30**, 38-39
Volume
    definition, **30**
    fixed vs. variable costs, 38,
        39
    indirect costs and, 41
    payer mix analysis, **58**
    in profit formula, 20, 23, **23**
    trend reporting, 112

658.048
W221

96832

LINCOLN CHRISTIAN COLLEGE AND SEMINARY

3 4711 00149 3248